Witnesses of These Things

Witnesses of These Things

Faithfulness Here and Now

J. AARON MILLER

CASCADE *Books* • Eugene, Oregon

WITNESSES OF THESE THINGS
Faithfulness Here and Now

Copyright © 2024 J. Aaron Miller. All rights reserved. Except for brief quotations in critical publications or reviews, no part of this book may be reproduced in any manner without prior written permission from the publisher. Write: Permissions, Wipf and Stock Publishers, 199 W. 8th Ave., Suite 3, Eugene, OR 97401.

Cascade Books
An Imprint of Wipf and Stock Publishers
199 W. 8th Ave., Suite 3
Eugene, OR 97401

www.wipfandstock.com

PAPERBACK ISBN: 978-1-6667-6715-5
HARDCOVER ISBN: 978-1-6667-6716-2
EBOOK ISBN: 978-1-6667-6717-9

Cataloguing-in-Publication data:

Names: Miller, J. Aaron, author.

Title: Witnesses of these things : faithfulness here and now / J. Aaron Miller.

Description: Eugene, OR : Cascade Books, 2024 | Includes bibliographical references.

Identifiers: ISBN 978-1-6667-6715-5 (paperback) | ISBN 978-1-6667-6716-2 (hardcover) | ISBN 978-1-6667-6717-9 (ebook)

Subjects: LCSH: Christianity—21st century. | Christianity—Forecasting. | Christianity and culture. | Theology.

Classification: BR121.2 .M482 2024 (paperback) | BR121.2 M482 (ebook)

VERSION NUMBER 021224

Scripture quotations are from New Revised Standard Version Bible, copyright © 1989 National Council of the Churches of Christ in the United States of America. Used by permission. All rights reserved worldwide.

For Kate, my co-conspirator, who teaches me every day what it looks like to live with intention and faithfulness.

Contents

Acknowledgments | ix
Introduction | xi

Chapter 1
Good News? | 1

Chapter 2
A Cruciform Church | 12

Chapter 3
Repentance | 34

Chapter 4
Forgiveness of Sins | 50

Chapter 5
Ascension | 81

Chapter 6
Within and Without | 90

Conclusion | 103

Bibliography | 107

Acknowledgments

I HAVE ALWAYS ASSUMED that this would be the hardest part of writing a book, and I feel vindicated in that belief as I attempt to think of all those who have played a part in this project. It would be impossible to name everyone. I am extremely lucky.

I am grateful to my parents, Paul Miller and Diane Walker, Susan Mabey and Katherine Noel, who not only pastored me and taught me about this vocation through their faithfulness and witness, but also instilled in me a love of learning and reading broadly.

I am thankful to the congregations of Kingsway-Lambton United Church (Etobicoke, Ontario), Faith Memorial United Church (Florenceville, New Brunswick), Faith Centennial United Church (Selkirk, Ontario), and University Hill United Church (Vancouver, British Columbia), for the grace and patience each community offered and continues to offer, as I try to be faithful in this pastoral call.

One of the great gifts of where I am is getting to hang around the Vancouver School of Theology, and I am grateful to President Rev. Dr. Richard Topping, and the staff and faculty for regularly letting me interlope on events in their communal life. It is not a stretch to say that this book may not exist were it not for the support and encouragement of Rev. Dr. Jason Byassee, and Rev. Dr. Ross Lockhart.

The insights and influence of countless friends undergird this whole project. I am particularly thankful to Simon LeSieur, Andria Irwin, Heather Joy James, Stevan Mirkovich, Daniel Martin, Ryan Slifka, Alex Wilson, Andrew Stephens-Rennie, Ingrid Hartloff Brown, Michelle Slater, and Rob Crosby-Shearer for your regular witness to God's goodness and grace in the beauties and challenges of ministry.

I'm thankful to everyone at Cascade who has had a hand in bringing this to life.

ACKNOWLEDGMENTS

I'm grateful for my sons, Levi and Jude, whose love and laughter remind me daily that there is nothing more important than the people who God has entrusted to us. Above all, I am thankful to my wife, Kate, who not only patiently read through every word of my manuscript, making it better as she went, but, in so many ways, tends the space that allows our family to grow more faithfully in the Way of Jesus. Thank you forever. I love you.

Introduction

THERE'S A QUIP FLOATING around social media about how people are leaving the church but not leaving Jesus. Occasionally, a video will surface of someone—usually a twentysomething—explaining why they "love Jesus but hate religion." Something about the shape of Christian community in the West can't seem to be reconciled with the table-flipping, poor-loving, life-changing, sword-not-peace fire of the gospel that people encounter in Jesus. Particularly in the murky wake of the 2016 American election, much "church news" has been concerned with the mass exodus of young people from evangelical churches in disillusionment and disbelief that their siblings and parents in faith could possibly have elected someone who so wholeheartedly embodies a gospel antithesis, and they used God-language to do it. Apparently young peoples' distaste for the traditions that they grew up in is more sociological than theological. They often echo Gandhi's sentiment that Christ he could get down with, but Christians are rather more trying.[1]

In some cases, the problem is that "youth look to the church to show them something, someone, capable of turning their lives inside out and the world upside down. Most of the time we have offered them pizza."[2] But it's not just youth. Many churches are entirely missing Gen-Xers, and it's not a given that their parents are showing up anymore, either. Even people who have been raised in the church, from committed Christian families, are absenting.[3] And to the degree that we've provided no more than snacks and games, or reduced our theology to sound bites and inspirational quotes, or simply relegated the Spirit who raises the dead to the limited realm of

---

1. Gandhi is quoted as saying, "I like your Christ, but not your Christianity." See "Mahatma Gandhi Says He Believes."

2. Creasy Dean and Foster, *God-bearing Life*, 9.

3. Barna, "Only 10%."

INTRODUCTION

whatever we think is possible, we are guilty of shortchanging our people. We're guilty of shortchanging *God's* people. It's no wonder they leave. I'm sympathetic to that impulse to get out. I get it. I think it's misguided, but I get it.

There are many times when I wish God would have chosen something more efficient and sexier than the church, something less messy, complicated, fickle, painful, and disappointing. But it seems clear that, by Divine design, we can't follow Jesus alone. And I'm willing to risk the possibility that God's plan might outstrip my frustrations and disillusionments. What's more, communities of sinners caught up in God's grace, and working to embody something like an appropriate response to that grace has been the shape of God's work in the world since the first Easter morning. The local congregation still seems to be "the core element in the strategy of the Holy Spirit for providing human witness and physical presence to the Jesus-inaugurated kingdom of God in this world."[4]

This witness is what's at stake. If people really are leaving the church but not Jesus, we've got a big problem. Because Jesus is expecting the church to be the Body that bears witness to him, embodies his will and way in the world. It's the only thing we exist for. If we're committed to anything less, we might as well lock the doors. I'm convinced that God will get the world God wants, whether we are faithful or not. But if we care about anything more interesting than preserving the institutions and structures we've created and loved, we'll take note.

This is a book about the church, for those who love and lead the church. Particularly as a part of the limb of the Body I care especially about: mainline Protestantism. It's been noted that the term "mainline" is notoriously hard to pin down. But what I mean is the collective group of liberal protestant denominations that have been a part of the social fabric in both Canada and the United States for generations. They might be called "establishment churches"—traditions that tend to hold educated clergy and liberal commitments, both theologically and socially, as especially important. They would tend to self-identify as *not* "evangelical"—another notoriously slippery term, and one I think we gave up too easily. In Canada, "mainline" would typically include the United Church of Canada, Presbyterian Church in Canada, and Anglican Church of Canada, and we would likely include some Lutherans and some Baptists. In the US, the standard list includes the Episcopal Church, Presbyterian Church (USA), northern Baptist churches,

---

4. Peterson, *Practice Resurrection*, 11.

INTRODUCTION

United Church of Christ, United Methodist Church, Evangelical Lutheran Church, and the Disciples of Christ.[5]

The numbers suggest that while these traditions are in one sense "established"—most towns and cities across the continent are marked by their historical presence and influence—in another and rather more serious sense they are rapidly dwindling, almost universally and in every way. There are a number of reasons for this, some of which are beyond our control and some of them are self-inflicted and deserved. That said, I want to insist that the mainline church is a voice and a space the world desperately needs, and a gospel witness that God is not done with.

Some Assumptions

This would be a much longer book if I fully addressed everything that needs attention paid to it. And certainly, anyone who sets out to talk about something as expansive as the church does so with some assumptions in tow. I want to briefly address three that I'm bringing:

1. My experience is mostly in the mainline church (in Canada), and I think the world needs us.
2. The church in the West is at a crucial but hopeful point in its history.
3. The Bible is essential for Christian witness.

I grew up in the largest Protestant denomination in Canada.[6] For the first half of my life, my parents were my pastors. I came of age at denominational camps, both as a camper and a counsellor. The United Church of Canada (UCC) baptized, confirmed, and finally—in an unexpected twist—ordained me. I had a short, unsuccessful attempt at rebellion in my early twenties. I've flirted with other denominations, other iterations, other visions of the church, some of whom I still have a bit of a crush on. But I've always come back. The UCC is in many ways my spiritual home. It worked—still works—for me. But, based on the church attendance statistics, the United Church of Canada is clearly not for everybody.

---

5. For a fascinating study of the mainline church in the USA, which rings frequently true in Canada, see Coffman, *Christian Century*.

6. The United Church of Canada is an amalgamation of Methodist, Presbyterian, and Congregationalist denominations formed in 1925.

INTRODUCTION

Of course, no one church or expression needs to be for every Christian. Even the churches we encounter in Scripture seem to have their own flavors. I have no trouble imagining that the folks in Colossae couldn't stand the Corinthian liturgy; the Ephesian congregations probably hated the kind of music the Philippian church played; the Romans surely rolled their eyes at the Jamesian social-justice nuts. I believe that God's impulse is toward particularity. We don't all have to respond to what God's up to in the same way.

As well, in the death gasps of Christendom—that stretch of time when whole cultures were at least nominally Christian, when we could count on passive reception of basic Christian teachings—and with increased multicultural engagement, it shouldn't come as a great surprise that lots of people have absented, thrown off nominal faith, and given up on institutions that sometimes feel comically past their best-before date. Without social pressure—both positive and negative—to be connected to a church, it's not all that unexpected that lots of folks have decided not to be. I'm not sure that decline was inevitable. But it's not surprising.

Still, many United Church of Canada and other mainline congregations continue to be places where people find faith that they can sink their teeth into, a faith that takes seriously our doubts and fears, and that compels us to live differently in the world as a testimony to the grace we have received in Christ. Many of our congregations are communities where those weary of "deconstruction"—unraveling the faith of their youth—find space to reconstruct on a faithful foundation. For lots of folks, my denomination has been a place where they have been allowed to be fully themselves *and* be committed to the will and Way of Jesus, in ways other expressions of church won't allow.

In the UCC, we call ourselves a "non-credal" church. That's a bit weird for a denomination that has its own creed.[7] But what we mean is that you don't have to believe exactly like us to get in on this thing. If you can say the Apostles' Creed unreservedly, or only with your fingers crossed behind your back, or if you choke on the first line, you're welcome here. And we'll give you some bread and wine because it's Jesus himself who invites you to the table.

It's a beautiful vision, that's not without its challenges. We've often been very good at saying what we're not—that is, not like those "conservative, closed-minded churches up the road"—than saying what we are.

---

7. United Church of Canada, "New Creed."

INTRODUCTION

I've been in denominational meetings where to say the name of Jesus with conviction is an absurdly suspicious, if not dangerous thing to do. (And not in a "these people are turning the world upside down" kind of way.)[8]

I've had my desire to deal seriously with God get subsumed by self-righteous gatekeeping. I recall when I was a student, on internship, being on retreat with a group of other students and their supervisors. We were in the process of spending an awfully long time setting up the parameters for what was appropriate and expected in this season of our preparation for ministry. We had a good long list of things like how to have good boundaries, how to give and receive criticism, and a bunch of other guidelines that would be appropriate for any other organization of reasonably mature adults. Finally, one of the leaders asked something to the effect of "What about God in all this?" To which I blurted, "Oh yeah, *Him!*"

This was met immediately with a blustering "*Excuse me?!*" from one of the supervisors in the room. The problem was unquestionably with my unabashed use of the masculine pronoun. I have absolutely no doubt that if I'd said, "Oh yeah, *Her!*" (which I could comfortably have done) I would have been met with approving smiles and nods. As though it's okay to talk about God, provided one does so within the narrow confines of a myopic form of liberalism.

On the other hand, I've also been in rooms full of clergy and lay leaders where saying the name of Jesus with conviction, inviting people seriously into the presence of God, brings an audible sigh of relief—like we've been given permission to talk about this thing that we all, at some point, committed our lives to. We can even admit to believing in some of it, though we may express that belief in different ways. That variety of expression can even be one of our gifts.

The Church in the West Is at a Crucial but Hopeful Point

Anyone paying attention can see that in my denomination we have been closing a whole lot more churches every year than we've opened. It would be foolish to suggest that there is one consistent reason for this. I recall in my first pastoral charge, one of the patriarchs remarking that in that rural area, there were churches built "a buggy ride away" from everyone. Of course, that assumes a local church attendance that is nearly mythological at this point. However, it means that in that area there were, at one point,

---

8. Acts 17.

INTRODUCTION

five United Churches (or antecedent congregations) within ten kilometers. The number at least doubled within another ten kilometers. Even without counting the two Church of Christ congregations, the Baptist, Roman Catholic, and Dutch Reformed churches, that's a lot of churches for one area. In many cases, it makes logistical sense to amalgamate congregations. It might be good stewardship of resources. Sometimes, closures are the next faithful step in God's mission. But often the reasons are less noble.

Even if we could keep every church open, we are not training nearly enough clergy to compensate for the wave of retirement of many baby boomers, which is starting to affect just about every sector of our culture. There is a catastrophic clergy shortage that is already starting to lay bare the challenges of doing church like we've always done. The denominational strategy has been to change our polity, the fruit of which remains to be seen but is not inspiring confidence on the ground. Sadly, my home denomination is not any different than any other denomination in Canada—or anywhere in the West. As of 2020, around a third of Presbyterian Church in Canada congregations were without clergy and not seeking to call clergy, largely due to size and financial limitations.[9]

But this is not going to be a book about church decline. It won't be about numbers, fiscal or physical. Jesus didn't seem to be all that interested in numbers. He was prepared to let folks walk, if that's what they wanted to do.[10] He tells us to count the cost, and bail if it's too high.[11] He was bold to suggest that two or three of us is plenty of material for God to work out the kingdom on earth, as in heaven.[12] On the other hand, a faithful witness often brings about the world's curiosity—and when that happens, people seem to want to join in. Once in a while they'll flood in.[13] So numbers tell a story, but they never tell the whole story. My friend, Jason Byassee, says that Christians need to "count weird." We're not just looking to draw a crowd; heaven's metrics aren't like ours.

What really matters is people caught up in God's restorative grace and bearing witness to it in faithful response, in the ordinary and everyday places we find ourselves. We need communities of people—small ones and big ones—ready to embrace the gospel's peculiar call to be strange in the

9. *Acts and Proceedings*, 200–210.
10. John 6:66.
11. Luke 14:28–30.
12. Matt 18:20.
13. Acts 2:47.

world, for the sake of the world that God wants. And we're at a point, being largely disregarded by the surrounding culture, where we can be strange again. We are under no obligation to mirror the world around us or prop up ways of being in the world that are dehumanizing and destructive.

This requires a holy imagination about what the church is for, who it's for, and what it means to live as though we believe that it's not the Church of God that has a mission, but the God of mission who has a church.[14] We need to join the saints in every generation who have believed this; and we need to let ourselves be shaped for God's redemptive purposes in our time and place, wherever that is.

Unshackled from the expectations of the world around, we're free to explore what it might mean to let God do abundantly far more than we have asked or imagined in some time.

The World Needs the Mainline

Denominations like mine that used to have social and even political sway don't anymore. At least, not like we used to. I have heard stories of politicians at every level of government seeking wisdom and support from mainline clergy. We used to get invited to pray at the opening of all sorts of social events. When my wife and I were engaged, and I had just begun seminary, a librarian friend rescued a book from the discard pile for her. It is called *How to Marry a Minister*. First published in 1968, it contains the rationale for why someone might want to marry a minister, and strategy for how to go about landing a clergy spouse. The author, a Methodist minister's wife, ranks being married to an ordained minister right up there with marriage to doctors and lawyers, as far as social standing goes! It is hard not to read it as a work of satirical comedy, though the author is absolutely serious. It is even harder to imagine that the local library would purchase it so that the general public would have access. It is no trouble at all to imagine why nobody was checking it out. It's not just that our numbers are down, but we are no longer the voice of authority or morality or even prophecy that we once were. We're not part of the public imagination of how things are. What used to be mainline is now sideline.[15] To lots of folks, we're a quaint relic. Many won't give us that.

---

14. Moltmann, *Church in the Power*, 64.
15. I borrow this phrase from Rev. Dr. Edwin Searcy.

INTRODUCTION

For many of us who have stuck with the church, the faithful who keep showing up, it's not always entirely clear why we do what we do. We tend not to articulate the point of our collective selves. We know what we do when we're together:

- Worship
- Attend to divine presence
- Rest in the stability and comfort of liturgy
- Deepen our discipleship, committing ourselves afresh, reorienting ourselves to the One in whom we live and move and have our being
- Serve and love our neighbors

People arrive at churches for any number of reasons—often essential reasons. But for lots of congregations, especially those that can remember a different time in the life of the church, it's a disorienting season. Week over week, so much is familiar. But it's undeniable that something is entirely different. Many of us feel or have felt like we're "lost in the house we grew up in."[16]

Still, I was ordained in 2010, long after the doom and gloom of church decline was ingrained in our cultural consciousness. And every spring, we celebrate the ordination of a handful of people, often younger than me, all of whom seem to have some idea of what they're getting into. We may not be preparing enough clergy to support every congregation in the country, but undeniably God continues to call people at various ages and stages to lead and serve this limb of Christ's body. And I think that's because we still have something to offer. God's not done with us.

Although I've spent most of my life in and around the United Church of Canada (I was in seminary *in utero*), I have a relatively broad experience of Christian witness and practice. As a teenager I hung around with charismatics; I'm pretty fluent in evangelical; I've spent time with Roman Catholics, United Methodists, and recently I've been carousing with Anabaptists. I've attended conferences with non-denoms, and am currently participating in an online project with an Eastern Orthodox friend. I heard my call to ordained ministry through an Alpha Course.[17] All this helps me hold my denominationalism lightly, and I certainly know there are other

---

16. Root, *Pastor*, 3.
17. See Alpha Canada, https://alphacanada.org/.

options whose pastures sometimes look rather greener than my own. I also know that they have their own peculiar temptations and regrets.

But I do care about the particular expression of Jesus's Way that nurtured me. And I believe that it can be—even, ought to be—a gift to a culture badly in need of good news alternatives to much of what is on offer all around us.

It's among mainliners that I've learned most intensely that theology and practice go together: that social justice isn't an add-on, or a subcategory of Christian witness—it's not a woke lefty conspiracy to undermine the church, but essential to it. The mainline has a history of faithful and prophetic political engagement that's worth maintaining and reinvigorating. It's the mainline that taught me that our contexts, our lives, our bodies, and our stories are not incidental to the gospel, but integral to working out God's purposes in this God-beloved world.

Of course, growing up and working mostly within one denomination means that we can assume I have blind spots. The UCC is predominantly populated by people of European descent, like me. Because we are not an international denomination (like Presbyterians or United Methodists), we are less influenced by the expressions of church that are bearing fruit in other parts of the world, and among other cultures. These are realities that temper my understanding of the church and what we're called to; they shape the biases that I bring to any ecclesial conversation. Acknowledging my denominational bias, I do hope that what follows will be valuable for anyone, and any community, eager to think through what it means to bear witness to the gospel as we move through the third decade of the twenty-first century.

In any case, the body needs its many parts, each doing what it's made to do. The mainline has in its DNA the combination of evangelical purpose and social concern that is essential for a fulsome witness to the will and Way of Jesus, in and for the world. We have not always lived into those essentials, or we have overprized one way or the other, but they remain part of who we are.

Every church, everywhere, is there because some group of Christians felt it was necessary to be in that place, to gather in worship and service—each one was a church plant at some point, eager to engage its neighborhood in the name and Way of Jesus, often expanding expectations of what that looks like. We're still meant for that. Leaning into it will help us faithfully

INTRODUCTION

discern God's call and claim on us, in this time and place. We might even turn the world upside down in the process.[18]

The Bible Is Essential for the Church

When the Eiffel Tower was built as the entrance to the 1889 World's Fair, it was a monument to modernism and industrial power, its stark frame symbolizing the ever-upward reach of a mechanical future. But it also gave the world an unanticipated gift. As the tallest man-made structure to that point, it offered for the first time—for everyone other than a handful of pilots and hot air balloonists—a view of the world truly from above. It was the first time that ordinary people could look out on the familiar from a truly new vantage.[19]

What from the ground might have seemed quite random was suddenly pattern and patchwork. The noise and motion of everyday life was rendered orderly, the lines and blocks coherent arrangements. No more mystery around corners, but a clear view of one street to the next; an ability to see what was previously hidden. People would have experienced the world in a whole new way, nearly as impactful as the first pictures of earth from space. The familiar was seen freshly.

Twice, in Luke's account of things, the resurrected Jesus explains himself to his disciples, what God has done in and through him, through the Scriptures.[20] His first resurrection task is to reestablish within them a biblical imagination for how things are.[21] The law, prophets, and psalms, along with the witness of the early church in the New Testament, are the only way to begin to understand who and how Jesus is for us and for all things, and what that means here and now. Jesus's teaching also gives us an interpretive frame for understanding how it is that we are meant to engage the Scriptures. It reminds us, first of all, that the Bible is authoritative for the church because—and only because—it points to Jesus. Jesus is the Word of God, toward whom, in cahoots with the Holy Spirit, the Bible points.[22] As Christians, we are meant to read and engage the Bible christologically.

---

18. Acts 17.
19. Hughes, "Shock of the New."
20. Luke 24:27, 45.
21. Mullins, *Enjoying the Bible*, 46.
22. John 1:1.

INTRODUCTION

I wonder, as Jesus explains the Scriptures from Moses to Malachi, opening the law and the prophets and the prayers for the disciples, if they aren't experiencing a change in perspective in the world of the Scriptures, similar to those who first looked out over Paris from the Eiffel Tower. To be clear: I don't want to read elevation as superior, but simply a new way of seeing. The life of the Scriptures on the ground is not negated by this new view. Indeed, the new view makes no sense without the familiar one. But it does start to make sense of things in a new way, in the company of Jesus, crucified and risen—a way that was not previously possible.

Walter Moberly points to the example of great literature's capacity to shape the view of the works that came before it and indeed helped to shape it. For instance, we understand eighteenth-century literature differently when we look at it through Jane Austen's writing from the nineteenth.[23] A similar illumination happens when we experience the Hebrew Scriptures through Jesus. Suddenly a world that has total integrity on its own is understood in a fresh way. The life, death, resurrection, and ascension of Jesus brings new depth to Genesis 3 or 12, to Joshua or Job, Isaiah, or Jeremiah. Take away that view and we still know the world clearly. We still know a promise-making, promise-keeping God; we're still in the company of the one who sets captives free, and heals the sick, and raises the dead; we can still recognize the God who gives of Godself relentlessly for the sake of his beloved people.

But through Jesus we see connections we never saw before. We see patterns that escaped our awareness. We see an order and purpose that would not otherwise have been clear. And it should go without saying—because Jesus says it, not to mention every other New Testament writer—that, vice versa, the Hebrew Scriptures are the only way to make sense of this crucified Jew standing, eating, talking among us, and sending us into the world.

A brief look at Genesis 3, specifically verse 15, can help us think about how this works elsewhere. This moment follows the eating of the forbidden fruit of the Tree of the Knowledge of Good and Evil. It's after the temptation to be as gods, instead of beloved creatures, has been disastrously succumbed to. Everything is unravelling in this world that was made to be good and very good. The rebellious serpent has got its way.

Then God makes some pronouncements. God starts, not with Adam and Eve, but with the serpent: the bringer of rebellion and brokenness. God tells the serpent that there will be enmity between him and a descendent of

---

23. Moberly, *Old Testament*, 158.

INTRODUCTION

Eve. The descendent will crush the head of the serpent, and the serpent will strike his heel. In other words, the one who will put an end to the rebellion and destruction instigated by the serpent will be a "wounded victor."[24] He will undo what the serpent has done, but not without cost. In the shadow of the cross, it does not take a great stretch of imagination to think about this christologically.[25] This promise, on the first pages of Scripture, that the destructor will be destroyed—and implicitly, what was torn apart will be restored—gives us an imagination for what has been accomplished through Jesus's death, and what is possible in the light of his resurrection.

Perhaps that's a good goal for what follows: an imagination for what's possible, through Christ, in us—wherever and whenever we are. What's *possible*. Not what's probable. Not what we can naturally imagine. Not what's likely under the circumstances, or if we try hard enough. But what's possible in the company of God, who does *more* than we can ask or imagine.[26]

It seems a little odd for a pastor to have to say that the Bible matters. For some limbs of the body, this will seem ridiculously obvious, but not always in mine. Frankly, studies show that even within those expressions that elevate the Bible above anything else, a whole lot of people don't actually read it.[27] So maybe mainliners are just more obvious about ambivalence toward the Scriptures.

Of course, *how* the Bible matters, matters. As inheritors of modernist scientific understandings of how things are, and the pervasive notion that what can be known, what is *true*, can only be arrived at by cool objectivity, we can be tempted to treat Scripture with a similar rigidity. We can be tempted to assume that the Bible is largely a series of instructions, commands, and requirements set in stone, which leads either to a truncated engagement, or throwing our hands up in frustration and walking away.

But Scripture is not meant to be read with the same dispassionate lens as we might bring to an operating manual for an appliance. Christians are committed to the promise that the Word is living and active, not always true in the same way, not frozen in time or pinned down by preconceived ideas or inherited beliefs. Anyone who has read and meditated on the Bible over years knows the feeling of reading a familiar passage as if for the first

---

24. I am indebted to The Bible Project for this insight.
25. Luke 23, for instance.
26. Eph 3:21–22.
27. Gibson, "How Much Do Evangelicals."

INTRODUCTION

time. The words themselves are not different, but the way that they are true in this moment or season is.

It's been said that you don't have to be a poet to be a Christian, but it helps.[28] In order to hear the Spirit's persistent, beckoning whisper, we have to resist the urge to constrict the authority of Scripture to the black-and-white words on the page. We actually have to get into it, chew it over, sometimes wrestle a blessing out of it. Treating it with dogged literalism will demand impossible mental gymnastics to flatten soaring paradoxes that are meant to be there—a feature, not a bug. On the other hand, treating it simply as an ancient text to be studied like any other literature often requires dissecting it in ways that explore the component parts but lose all the life in the process.

Reading the Bible is hard. Living into its authority is a spiritual discipline, not a matter of superimposing "plain Bible truth" on every situation and circumstance, as if the situation or circumstance itself doesn't really matter. Nor is it meant only for our inspiration or edification, which would require ignoring anything troubling, confronting, or demanding. It's a relational Word, through which God speaks and expects a response. And relationship is hard. It's easy to opt out.

But the Bible is not optional for the church—or any congregation—that wants to be active participants in God's redeeming work in the world. In fact, we can't even begin to articulate what "God's redeeming work in the world" is, without the biblical witness. Except that we allow the Scriptures to shape our imagination *and* have meaningful authority in our lives—individually and corporately—we may do something, maybe even something interesting, but there is no guarantee that it will be what God's doing. And mixed in with all my assumptions is the conviction that whatever God is up to is infinitely more interesting that whatever we might come up with on our own.

A Commission

So, the mainline can be a bit nebulous. It's sometimes not entirely clear what we're doing here. If we believe that Jesus is still calling, what's he calling us to? If we believe the Spirit is still moving, into what wilderness might

---

28. This is Will Willimon's interpretation of W. H. Auden's poem, "For Christopher Isherwood and Chester Kallman," confirmed via email (February 9, 2023). Willimon, *Undone*, 79.

she be driving us? If we're actually in cahoots with the God who delights to do new things, how can we have eyes to see that newness clearly?

These are the sorts of questions that often roll around my pastoral heart. I don't think God calls us to preserve denominations, or even particular congregations. In the company of Jesus there's always the chance we'll be told to sell everything precious to us and get where he's going instead of where we'd rather be. At the same time, I'm convinced that we've buried our treasure, either as a way to preserve it, or to hide and protect it from cultured despisers. I'm increasingly eager to dig that treasure up, to sell out for the possibility that God actually trusts us to do something with it; to invest it in this God-beloved world and see what kind of a return we can get.

A few years ago, I stumbled across a passage of Scripture that I'd read lots of times before, as if for the first time. It's captured my imagination for what it means to be the church, to be a people claimed by the name and Way of Jesus ever since. It's not a church growth strategy (though wild faithfulness tends to draw a crowd),[29] but it is a framework for faithfulness that allows us to take our times and places seriously as soil that God wants to play in; it compels us to deal with the people in front of us, as those for whom God would give everything; it woos us toward the hard and challenging corners of our world as those who walk in the extravagant hope that God's going to get the world God wants—and that God created it all good in the first place, and it will be good and *very* good again.

In Luke 24:47–48, the risen Jesus tells his disciples what will shape their vocation as his followers: *the proclamation of repentance and forgiveness of sins, in his name.* These things, he says, will define Christian witness. That's the framework for faithfulness. The challenge for us is to understand just what Jesus meant by it. How can we hear this commission well, when words like "repentance" and "forgiveness" and "sin" are words that often create barriers and bindings, instead of boundaries for true freedom? And once we've heard it well, how are we to bear witness?

---

29. Acts 2.

Chapter 1

Good News?

At its origins, Christianity's surprise was a person, Jesus the Messiah, crucified and raised. To receive this surprise and rebroadcast it, the earliest Christians discovered that they had to tell the story of everything. And the story put them in the world in a particular way: Christians know that they live in a time where they serve Jesus in a still-fallen world that is being newly created even now, awaits his final return, and hopes for the eternal healing of all that is.[1]

> We declare to you what was from the beginning, what we have heard, what we have seen with our eyes, what we have looked at and touched with our hands, concerning the word of life. . . .
>
> 1 JOHN 1:1

I RECENTLY ATTENDED AN online church service that was experimenting with real-time closed captioning. It's a remarkable bit of technology, though not without its challenges. On this particular Sunday, when the preacher proclaimed with great passion that "Jesus was anointed to preach *good news!*" the bottom of the screen read: "Jesus was annoyed to be pretty good news."

---

1. Rowe, *Christianity's Surprise*, 3.

I think that's hilarious. And convicting. It's weird how the Holy Spirit works.

I don't think that Jesus spends his days annoyed at the church, though the Gospels aren't shy about the possibility.[2] We should probably pay attention to the letter to the lukewarm Laodiceans, in the Revelation to St. John.[3] There's a chance that our actions are nauseous to the Lord. Those passages notwithstanding, I'm more inclined to believe that Jesus's default is, "Forgive them; they don't know what they're doing."[4] But, I do think the Holy Spirit used that technical glitch to get under my skin. Even though I laughed as those words were juxtaposed against the preacher's proclamation, I can't help but feel that we have too often reduced the wondrous and world-inverting claim of the Gospel of Jesus Christ to "pretty good news." "Pretty good news" is something that we can sneak out the side door of the sanctuary, usually with just the parts we like. It's easily reduced to meme-worthy one-liners and pious sound bites.

Unfortunately, "pretty good news" is not the biblical witness to the state of things in the light of Jesus.[5] The storytellers and letter writers, the pastors and prophets of the New Testament, are extravagant in their insistence that what God has done in the life, death, resurrection, and ascension of Jesus of Nazareth is nothing short of the very best of all possible news. This is news that makes *all things* new.[6] This is reconciliation and wholeness for a fractured world. This is hope beyond hope, peace beyond understanding, life that is *truly* life.[7] The gospel is the news that evil, brokenness, failure, fear, not only won't get the last word on us, but everything opposed to God's good way for this beloved world will choke on its tongue.[8] *Every* tear will be wiped away, and *every* hunger—including all our deepest longings for love and justice and righteousness—will be satisfied. While what's wrong suffocates on its own lifelessness, what's right is going to sing with the choirs of heaven.

There are any number of reasons that an increasing number of people in Western culture can't or won't be bothered to get out of bed on a Sunday

2. Mark 9:19 and parallels.
3. Rev 3:14–22.
4. Luke 23.
5. Daniel and Copenhaver, *Odd and Wondrous Calling*.
6. Rev 21:5.
7. Heb 3:15; Phil 4:7; 1 Tim 6:19.
8. Rom 8:38–39.

morning to hear this news. But at least part of the reason is that many of us who believe it have given the impression that the gospel is more like spiritual wallpaper on the walls of our nicely ordered lives, than the new foundation that completely rearranges them.[9] And wallpaper trends come and go. We in the mainline have often lived as though the gospel is "pretty good news." A pleasant spiritual embellishment, a touch of divinity, adorning whatever else it is we're doing.

We are tempted to do this at least in part because "pretty good news" makes very few, if any, demands on us. "Pretty good news" arrives without any threat of transformation, or loss, or—heaven help us—suffering.[10] "Pretty good news" can't grip us. It can't convict or challenge us. We can take it or leave it. It's certainly not worth ordering our schedules, or our finances, or our relationships around. It's a pleasant distraction, like a feel-good story between the wars and rumors of wars that make up most of our newsfeeds. "Pretty good news" is something we talk about easily and often in passing. It's not something we live. Because we are not meant to live "pretty good" lives.

But the gospel—the wildly good news of Jesus, crucified, risen, and reigning—demands to be lived. Beautifully and inconveniently so. We are promised that to be in Christ is both a way of life that is abounding in love and joy, and also difficulties and persecutions.[11] The gospel says that we are called, claimed, and commissioned by the One who is making all things, even us, new. That can't just be talked about, and it's not passing away.

I dare say that in my limb of the body of Christ, excess talking is not generally our problem. We tend to avoid too much gospel talk outside the appropriate places. We like the oft-quoted (and probably misattributed) Franciscan encouragement to "preach the gospel everywhere, and use words if necessary." In a similar vein, I have long loved St. Peter's encouragement to be prepared to speak of faith, should someone ask. And of course, we should talk about it; living the gospel does require a readiness to give account of our hope.[12] Good news demands to be shared, even proclaimed. Absolutely, we must learn or relearn how to speak the gospel freshly and

---

9. I'm indebted to Eric Hiestand for this image.
10. Matt 5:11.
11. Mark 10:30.
12. 1 Pet 3:15.

with conviction, wherever we find ourselves. If we don't tell folks, how will they know?[13]

Still, our testimony finds its proof in our living. What Jesus says and what Jesus does are the same thing, and he seems to expect the same thing of us. The Word always becomes flesh.[14] The church bears witness not to a new philosophy or a set of principles to which we give only our intellectual assent. The church bears witness to what we have *heard, seen, looked at,* and *touched.*[15] God's work in the world is tangible. We're invited to experience it in our bones, in our guts. And the church's invitation is for others to come and do the same.

I've often reflected on St. Paul's conviction that his work and ours is the "defense and confirmation of the gospel."[16] Defense *and* confirmation. Preaching *and* living as though what we preach is true. Sharing the good news *and* living in such a way that people might be able to see what's good about it.

Consider the holy circus that must have been the community we hear about in Acts 2: "Awe and wonder" grabbing hold of anyone paying attention. Signs of God's kingdom everywhere. Miracles around every corner—not the least of which was rich folks choosing downward mobility for the sake of their neighbors. Selling their stuff so they'd have more to give! *No poor among them*! Dinner parties every night. Songs of praise rising at all hours of the day; lives shaped by the rhythms of worship in the temple and at the kitchen table. And they had the goodwill of all the people (imagine that!).

And every day the Lord added to their numbers those who were being saved. This is important: they are *being* saved. This is not a one-off altar call, but a community learning to lean into the salvation that is theirs, caught up with the God of resurrection. Theirs is a journey out of the narrow possibilities of the world, and into the exceedingly wide space of God's goodness and grace. As they walk in this new way, they call others into the parade. That's what the church was meant to do.

I think this is what the church is still meant to do. But to do that, many of us need to listen again and hear not "pretty good news," but what is truly *good news*. The need for this fresh listening doesn't make us radically

---

13. Rom 10:14.
14. John 1:14.
15. 1 John 1:1.
16. Phil 1:7.

different from Christians at other times and elsewhere. We're not lagging behind our spiritual forebears in faith. For as long as there has been a church, Christians often shrugged off the wild claims of the gospel, the heavenward call of God in Christ, the cross-bearing Way of Jesus, for something else.[17] The great cloud of witnesses that has gone before can undoubtedly point at plenty of instances where the gospel has been the religious wallpaper of a nominally Christian culture, rather than the foundation of lives renewed, restored, and reclaimed for God and God's purposes.

That said, rehashing the spotted history of Christian witness is not necessary for us to recognize that this particular time in the history of the Western church is crucial.

On the one hand, and for a variety of reasons, the church in Europe and North America has seen a steady decline in attendance, adherence, and influence for quite a while now. No one inside or outside the church needs convincing that our so-called "glory days" are behind us.[18]

I was twelve years old when businesses were legally allowed to open on Sundays in Ontario where I grew up—including children's and youth sports clubs. Of course, this was not a lightly made decision and was surely the right one in a multicultural society. Forced closures on Sundays unjustly penalized people who were not Christian. And notably, if the business benefitted the government directly—like the Liquor Control Board of Ontario—they were allowed to remain open. However, the almost immediate decimation of many mainline Sunday schools and, indeed, congregations, as households had a choice to make between church and *just about anything else,* is hard to overstate.

---

17. Phil 3:14.

18. It's important to pay attention to the fact that most of the popular narratives of church decline are focused on European descendent denominations, specifically in Europe and North America. While it's true that those churches have been steadily waning in both attendance and influence for generations, the church in other parts of the world is flourishing. For example, The Vancouver School of Theology (VST), where my congregation rents chapel and office space, has developed partnerships with St. Andrew's seminary, Quezon City, in the Philippines, and Jakarta Theological Seminary, in Indonesia, because the church there is growing too quickly for local seminaries to support it. In the words of Rev. Dr. Richard Topping, president of VST, "Most of the problems with the church there have to do with growth." This is a radically different narrative. Making broad generalizations about the decline of the church, when that decline is affecting largely European-descendent, Western denominations is a vestige of Eurocentric colonialism, and is at least subtly, if not outright, racist.

It would be easy to blame the rise of a cultural secularism or argue that this is somehow the government's fault, except that the choice between church and anything else doesn't seem to have taken lots of people very long to make. I can't help but wonder if that's because the possibility of my kid making the NHL, or the chance to get in an extra round of golf, or brunch with friends, or, or, or, is more compelling than "pretty good news."

The saints in any given generation are not ultimately responsible for the choices made by those who have opted out. Faith can't be lived for someone else. But somewhere along the way, something has gone sideways. And it is easy to discern a kind of spiritual restlessness in both pews and pulpits.

Still, something pulls at us. Even if congregations are smaller than they used to be, every week many thousands of them continue to meet, continue to sing and pray, worship and study together. People are choosing to show up to and participate in the life and work of the church when they could easily—sometimes much more easily—do anything else. This is the flip side of this crucial time, in my mind. Every week, in many ways, forms, styles, and contexts, the church shows up, because we are still convinced that the gospel is not "pretty good news," but the hope of the world.

What's more, in many corners of the mainline there's a sense of faithful adventure. Now that we are much closer to the margins of our culture than in previous generations, we get to be weird again. One of my more adventurous colleagues managed to replant a closed United Church by wearing that weirdness on their sleeves—and putting it on their signs. Weird Church, in Cumberland, BC, is a vibrant group of spiritual (self-described) "weirdos" figuring out how to live the gospel in a strange land. They're doing what we all get to do now and what the church has been called to do since the beginning: bear witness to an alternative to "the way things are." We get to be "communities of contrast" again.[19] We can offer a way of being in the world that's odd enough that some folks might think to ask about it. There is no pressure to maintain the status quo. The church is not responsible for shaping good citizens. Increasingly, there is no social capital attached to church connection. The only reason to show up is to be caught up in something other than the life we would choose for ourselves, something more than we can ask or imagine.

Of course, the death gasp of Christendom has been more of a drawn-out sigh. And sure: some folks are always going to show up just for the

---

19. This is a phrase I borrow from Tim Dickau. See *Forming Christian*, 35.

community, or out of habit or obligation. Perhaps the good news is that God has often worked with far less noble motivations. But I don't really believe that that's enough to keep people showing up. Not when there are easier communities elsewhere, and more seductive things to occupy our time.

And what's more, I don't believe that most Christians are satisfied with the pervasive notion that our faith is limited to an hour or two of public worship each week, along with whatever devotions we manage to fit into our bloated and frantic schedules. My hunch, born of experience, is that people are eager to let the gospel be the all-consuming reality that it is. We want the church to be a "colony of heaven."[20] We want our regular prayer that God's kingdom would come *on earth as in heaven* to be more than mindless repetition.[21] So much more than paying bills until we die, we want the "life that is truly life" that the gospel promises.

We're just not always sure how to get in on that.

A Faithful Framework

I'm not always sure exactly how to get in on the life that the gospel promises, especially since I'm convinced that God is ready and willing to do *more* than we can do on our own. But I do think that Jesus has given us a framework that's part command and part invitation, which can help us work the gospel into our whole lives. At the tail end of Luke's gospel, Jesus, raised from the dead, shows up to his disciples. Luke tells us this:

> While they were talking about this, Jesus himself stood among them and said to them, "Peace be with you." They were startled and terrified, and thought that they were seeing a ghost. He said to them, "Why are you frightened, and why do doubts arise in your hearts? Look at my hands and my feet; see that it is I myself. Touch me and see; for a ghost does not have flesh and bones as you see that I have." And when he had said this, he showed them his hands and his feet. While in their joy they were still disbelieving and still wondering, he said to them, "Have you anything here to eat?" They gave him a piece of broiled fish, and he took it and ate in their presence.
>
> Then he said to them, "These are my words that I spoke to you while I was still with you—that everything written about me in

20. Peterson, *Practice Resurrection*, 12.
21. The Lord's Prayer. See Matt 6:9–13; Luke 11:2–4.

the law of Moses, the prophets, and the psalms must be fulfilled." Then he opened their minds to understand the scriptures, and he said to them, "Thus it is written, that the Messiah is to suffer and to rise from the dead on the third day, and that repentance and forgiveness of sins is to be proclaimed in his name to all nations, beginning from Jerusalem. You are witnesses of these things. And see, I am sending upon you what my Father promised; so stay here in the city until you have been clothed with power from on high."[22]

Up to this point, the resurrection has been all hearsay. The Emmaus road couple have burst in, breathlessly announcing that they've impossibly met Jesus. Peter, apparently, has seen him. Oh, and the women with their angel stories had mentioned something. But it's still not perfectly clear what's going on. So, it's hard to blame the disciples for standing around talking about Jesus. Even so, when Luke begins the post-Emmaus witness by telling us that the disciples were *talking about these things*, I can't help but think about so many board meetings, and church councils, and conferences, and sermons where mostly what happens is Jesus-talk.

The most useful preaching critique I've ever received came when I was settling into my current pastoral charge. It's on a university campus, and consequently many of the folks who make up the community are highly educated. I was eager to demonstrate how clever and competent I was. But someone who cares about me and the gospel told me that my sermons were really good, had strong content, sound theology, *and stopped just before God got a chance to speak*. Needless to say, my pride was hurt. But it was true. I was showing off my theological skills. I was vainly talking *about* God. And selling us all short in the process.

I don't think I'm alone in doing that. The Bible, at least, is full of instances when folks honor God with their lips but stop short of letting God get at their hearts. As often as not, we nod politely at wonder, tell of an overheard miracle, and then get back to the business at hand. We use words like "resurrection," we talk about the "promises" of our promise-keeping God. We even dare to proclaim that everything is new in the light of that first Easter morning and that we're all about that newness.

And yet, for many of us, not much seems all that new at all. We say these things, and then we carry on in what we're assured is the *real* world. We pay much more attention to the grey clouds of the news cycle than to the lightning strike of the gospel. We spend hours upon hours looking at

---

22. Luke 24:36–49.

our smartphones, and occasionally offer a sideways glance at the alternative story that God is writing even now.

We live in an information-obsessed world. This means that we have a tendency to "mistake the explanation for the thing itself."[23] Which is why we are tempted to talk *about* God, to explain the divine. But nowhere in the gospel does Jesus call his disciples to explain him. In fact, when it comes to talking about him, he instructs us explicitly not to plan ahead.[24] Instead, he over and over calls us to follow him: to do what he says and do what he does. The gospel is not an abstract concept to be untangled; it's a reality to be lived. All the Jesus-talk in the world will not make us faithful. Theology is important. Thinking well is important. Evangelism is important. But it only matters to the degree that it finds shape in our lives.

Still, I think it's fair to say that we talk for the same reasons those first disciples did: it's hard/confusing/too good to believe that it's true. And so, we talk—quietly and in the sanctioned places, mostly. We crunch numbers. We weigh options. We test out the reports of the faithful against the things we know for certain, because we've been taught them for forever.

But then, by grace, the most miraculous thing happens. *Jesus himself stood among them and said to them, "Peace be with you."* The church is bold to say, sometimes in spite of ourselves, that when we gather a few of us together, when we share some bread and wine, fill the font, anoint the sick, slump down in the ash heap and rise up to sing, Jesus himself will stand among us. We might expect him to criticize all our religious chatter, our doubts and fear, our failures and faithlessness. Instead, he says, "Peace."

And the chatter stops.

The chatter stops, as he moves us from talking in abstract to being witnesses of the way things really are. Among the first things Jesus does when he's raised from the dead is stop his disciples from talking about him, and insist that they *look at him*, bear witness. Our first task is not to talk about Jesus, to explain God's work, to say romantic things about the Holy Spirit. Our first task is to witness. To pay attention. Not talk; look and listen. See his hands and feet, his side. Then hear what he has to say, this Word made flesh.

And if we'll listen, this is what he tells us: First, his life, death, resurrection, and reign are not an isolated interruption in the world. No. He is

---

23. Mullins, *Enjoying the Bible*, 38.
24. Luke 12:12.

the *modus operandi* of the God whom the Scriptures sing, the God who calls and claims.

Christians are folks who point at something not-quite-graspable but, led by Scripture, sing of the God who longs to be known by us, and (Lord have mercy) through us. The story of Jesus, and the life of the church, only makes sense in the story of God with God's people—from Moses to the prophets, to the congregations that have echoed the psalms of praise and pain, horror and hope in every generation. The first thing that calms the disciples' idle chatter and tempers their fear is having their minds opened to understand the Scriptures.

The thing that begins in us a movement from talk to whole-life witness is an open-minded, soft-hearted, deep engagement with God's Word, from Genesis to Revelation.

The second thing Jesus tells the disciples is that "repentance and forgiveness of sins is to be proclaimed in [my] name to all nations. . . . You are witnesses of these things." This is the framework for faithfulness. The disciples have witnessed everything that Jesus now reminds them about—the outworking of the Scriptures, his suffering death, his third-day resurrection. But from here on, all of that will find expression in the living out of these two Christ-shaped realities: *repentance* and *forgiveness*, in his name, for the world.

Repentance and forgiveness are not words we are likely to put on our church banners and promo materials. They have fallen out of fashion, or been wielded in such a narrow and threatening way that they don't represent anything that could be called good news, let alone the "life abundant" that Jesus promises.[25] But in a time when the church is on uncertain footing, a time full of fear and doubt, when many churches are not living in abundance but sputtering in self-preservation mode, a recovery of these words and the depth of their meaning can orient us toward a future and faithful flourishing.

The case for keeping these now-unfamiliar words is that they are weird. As we think and talk and discern about what it means to be people living in the will and Way of Jesus—communities committed to living strange enough in this world now that when God gets the world God wants, we'll fit right in. These words are important precisely because they are jarring and uncommon. Part of translating the gospel in any given time and space is assuredly learning how to speak it in language that people understand.

---

25. 1 Tim 6:19; John 10:10.

That's good and important work, and a reminder that the gospel is meant to be accessible to "every language under the sun."[26] But in the wake of Christendom, we should also be aware that familiarity can breed apathy, which is often harder to overcome than contempt. The fact that "repentance" and "forgiveness of sins" don't roll easily off most peoples' tongues anymore gives them fresh potency.

What's more, sticking with these out-of-date words might serve to remind us that the church does not need to "change or die," as if what we really need is better branding and a different mission statement, or to simply get rid of everything that doesn't suit us anymore in order to be more relevant to the surrounding culture. Reflecting on "repentance and forgiveness of sins" is not seeking a new way of doing things. It's learning to rearticulate the strangeness of our faith—the holy irrelevance[27]—rather than make it conform to the patterns of the world around. It's to embrace the reality that this is the substance of our work and witness as followers of Jesus, and participants in his kingdom on earth as in heaven, and it has been since the beginning of the church. Part of our task as Christians today is to understand what Jesus meant by those words in context, and then let the Holy Spirit do whatever translating is necessary here and now.[28] And the local church is the primary place where that happens.

While they belong together, chapters 3 and 4 will look at each half of this command-invitation separately. After a brief look at the strange doctrine of the ascension in chapter 5, chapter 6 will be space to consider the practices that help shape us in the way of repentance and forgiveness. But before we get there, it is worth letting our gaze linger a while longer on Jesus, whose Way shapes all our ways.

---

26. Acts 2.

27. Nouwen, *In the Name of Jesus*, 35.

28. John 14:26. As Pete Davis puts it: "Indeed, what is static in successful movements is not the battle plan but the commitment to the movement's vision and values." *Dedicated*, 18.

Chapter 2

A Cruciform Church

Thus it is written, that the Messiah is to suffer
and to rise from the dead on the third day.

Luke 24:46

Then he said to them all, "If any want to become my followers, let them deny
themselves and take up their cross daily and follow me."

Luke 9:23

Whatever is done in the name of Jesus must be done in the Way of Jesus.

Such a statement should be so obvious that it makes us roll our eyes. Except that the church has always needed the reminder. Consider that the Corinthian church had to be reminded not to grab everything they could from the communion table, and to not get drunk in worship.[1] Or that the Christians that James was writing to—folks bearing the name of the One who insists time and again that his way messes with our familiar social arrangements—had to be told not to have special seating for rich folks.[2] Or that the pickpockets in the Ephesian church needed to be told that they

---

1. 1 Cor 11:17–22.
2. Jas 2:1–7.

really shouldn't do that anymore.³ The past two millennia are littered with glaring, occasionally horrific, instances of Christians doing things, *as Christians*, that don't look in any way Christlike. Sometimes we have learned our lesson, and sometimes certain temptations have been taken from us.

These days, instead of maturing into the image of God in which we are made, instead of getting after our divine vocation to love God and neighbor with trinitarian passion, we've regularly traded that commission for business plans and self-protection; we've absorbed a worldly fear of lack, instead of trusting in God's abundance; we've limited our possibilities to what is prudent and culturally appropriate, instead of risking the hope that God really will do more than we can ask or imagine. Instead of being an icon of God's dream for the world we have been an idol of the world's dreams for its gods.

An icon is something looked at and then through to something (for Christians, *someone*) greater, more, extravagantly beyond the thing immediately in front of us. An icon moves the eyes of our hearts beyond the thing itself.

An idol, on the other hand, is something that halts our gaze; it becomes the object of adoration and veneration; it points only to itself.⁴ Its aim is to capture our attention and hold it hostage.

The church is meant to be an *icon* of God's kingdom—the body revealing Christ's fullness,⁵ a glimpse of the way things will be when God gets the world God wants. We should never mistake our worship, our traditions, our work as the be-all and end-all. What we do should never point at what *we* do. What we do should always ultimately point to what God has done, is doing, and will do. All we are and have is meant to reveal the *moreness* of God. Life as the church should open us—and anyone who sees what we do—to surprise and wonder. A church in step with the spirit that blows where the spirit wills, will be a church eager for God to do more and other than we expect, in us and through us.

My friend Preston Pouteaux and his team lead their church in Chestermere, Alberta. They've embraced Dallas Willard's excellent advice that Christians should listen to what Jesus says, and then get together and try to do it. Preston recognized at one point that the dimensions of Chestermere, along the banks of a man-made lake, were about the same as the area of

---

3. Eph 4:28.
4. Dickau, *Forming Christian*, 156.
5. Eph 1:23.

Galilee in which Jesus spent most of his life. In other words, this suburb of Calgary was about as much space as Jesus needed for his ministry. This handful of kilometers, and the people who live there is sufficient to reveal the kingdom of God, in the local, particular, and attentive Way of Jesus.

So, the congregation of Lake Ridge Community Church have set about doing that by coming together to do what Jesus says to do: love God and neighbor with everything they've got. They regularly serve the community around them without any agenda beyond genuine care. They throw street parties without church signs. They spearhead advertising campaigns for their city without reference to themselves, simply because they think their place is worth loving. They plant gardens, and make spaces for youth, and host boxcar rallies and poetry-writing parties. They show up when tragedy strikes—whether among church members or not. They do it all without the bait-and-switch that makes so many people wary of the church. The goal is not to grow a church. The goal is to love their neighbors, to honor the image of God in them, because Jesus said to. They love their place and its people because God does.

Of course, the church has grown. But it's not the sort of place where you can get lost in a sea of fellow religious consumers. Instead, the Spirit takes their loaves and fishes and makes a feast. Their neighbors are regularly curious about why strangers would care for them. A group of people exuding love, learning to live with their guards down, doing the hard work of being in relationship—embodying another possibility than the closed-door, neurotically self-indulgent world we are so often confronted with—is magnetic.

Moreover, it flourishes because it's the stuff our souls need. It's the stuff we're made for, as people made in the image of God, made to reveal what God is up to in this beloved world. It's the "abundantly far more" that God wants to do in us and through us. It's what Jesus did, does, and will do. Moreover, life together in the Way of Jesus allows us to take the long view and commit to the slow work of creative restoration of the damaged and broken relationships and places around us.[6]

Whenever we stop at the level of our experience or expectation, we usually stop being an icon of God's kingdom, and become an idol of the world's kingdoms.[7] We often do so in the name of expediency or conve-

---

6. Pouteaux, *Bees of Rainbow Falls*.

7. "Kingdom" is a tricky word. It's outdated and patriarchal. Many people in my tradition prefer the term "kin-dom" to "kingdom," when referring to the world as it is and

nience. This is most obvious when the church is the agent of violence, literally or metaphorically. It's hard to reconcile (though we're awfully crafty, and so we try) the kinds of destruction done, presently and throughout history, in the name of the One who tells us to love our enemies and pray for our persecutors and be prodigal in our concern for the poor.

It should cause us whiplash when anyone is hurt in the name of the One who insists that it's the merciful and the peacemakers who are the blessed ones, the One who willingly died for love of the world—even for those who brutalized and nailed him to the cross.[8] Animosity and violence toward "others," however defined, is a sign that the church is captive to a different social project than the kingdom of God.[9]

Over the past several years, many people in my community and across Canada have been reeling at the revelation of hundreds of unmarked graves discovered at Indian residential schools across Canada.[10] We should not actually be surprised by this discovery. The Truth and Reconciliation Commission made clear that mass graves like this were not a probability, but a certainty.[11] Still, the news shocks and appalls. Most of us inside the church are left to wonder how this could have happened.

---

will be when God gets the world God wants. While I understand resistance to both the patriarchal and imperial implications of "kingdom," and the fact that it's antiquated, I still prefer it. And as much as the household ("kin") image is important for the pastors and preachers in Scripture, it should go without saying that, in context, that image assumed a head of the household. What's more, the foundational (anti-imperial) claim of the church is "Jesus is Lord." While in one sense the church is a body in which authority is levelled by grace, we must always insist on the good news that Jesus alone is the head, ruler, and king of the kingdom we're meant to embody. Anything else might be "pretty good news" but it won't change the world.

8. Matt 5:1–11, 43–44; Luke 23:34.

9. Winner, *Danger of Christian Practice*, 25.

10. Indian residential schools were the cooperative effort between the Canadian government and several Christian denominations, including the United Church of Canada, to westernize the indigenous children of this land. They were often taken violently from their families and far from their communities. They were stripped of their cultures and not allowed to speak their languages. While the intentions of individuals involved in this effort may be many and varied, it is now widely regarded as inexcusably racist and ultimately genocidal. The indigenous peoples of Canada continue to deal with the generational trauma inflicted by the policies and institutions that supported residential schools. The last one closed in 1996.

11. Truth and Reconciliation Commission Reports, https://nctr.ca/records/reports/#trc-reports.

But the answer may be as simple as the facts are wretched. Theologically speaking, the problem is sin; the profound breakdown of life-giving relationship for which we are made. However, with the benefit of hindsight we can see that the atrocity that is residential schools—the shape of that particular sin—is the result of the church consenting to be an idol for the culture that surrounded it. It's the church choosing to be an end in itself, a body that directly reflected and baptized the mores and ambitions of the world in which it found itself. This is the church caught up in the modernist, white supremacist confidence that there really is one ideal, divinely ordained, human culture—a belief that significantly undergirds the outworking of any colonialist project.[12]

Obviously, the facts of history require the church to confess and repent of our collective sin. The church should be a place where we name hard truths and choose another way. In some measure, if imperfectly, there have been efforts to do so. There have been public confessions and apologies offered, and some financial restitution made. My denomination works hard to address its own colonialist inclinations and recognize the essential contributions that indigenous people have made to our shared ministry. It seems hopeful that we may continue to turn from the sins of our collective past, at least where colonialism is concerned. While we're at it, we ought probably to confess *our own* self-assuredness. Experience should chasten our inclinations to assume that we will get it right this time, where others failed.

Still, trusting in God's grace, every generation that claims the name of Jesus has as its own work the task of discerning what it means to be a faithful witness to Jesus Christ. We may look back in horror at what some of our ancestors in faith did; and hopefully that horror keeps us from doing likewise. But at least as important is our own present willingness to live our lives in the light of the One whose ways and means are always a challenge to ours, whatever the time and place. Our culture may have different

---

12. It's almost certainly anachronistic to so cleanly divide "church" from "culture" in this case, as if the two were not, in many ways, mutually reinforcing. And of course, there are other factors, largely economic. But it does not take a great deal of imagination (or knowledge) to believe that robust trade could have happened without the decimation of indigenous cultures. For a similar interpretation of the relationship between Christianity and slavery in the American south see Winner, *Danger*, 79. It may be that my own beloved mainline denomination (and others like us) is more easily tempted to collude with the principalities and powers of the day. The United Church of Canada was created by an act of parliament. Our name proudly bears the country's name.

expectations and seductions, but we will be every bit as tempted toward them as the saints before us were.

Our current lack of political clout probably keeps us from certain temptations. It's hard to imagine today's Canadian government actively colluding with the church to further some mass project—for good or ill.[13] Even so, we're easily wooed. The culture around us captivates our attention. The age-old temptations of money, power, and knowledge still work on us. We still clamor after these things, make decisions based on them (either because we have them, or don't). We orient our life—individually and corporately—toward them.

The shape of the temptations may differ, but the truth is that the devil is not creative. Sin is never actually interesting. It's always dressed-up variations on tired themes. The things that tempt us are always, in the end, more boring than the things that Jesus calls us to.

In order to get to the things that are truly life-giving, generative, joyful, and abundant, we need to not just claim the name, but learn the *Way* of the One through whom and for whom all things are made—the truly creative One.[14] We're called to be *like* Jesus, to do what he does and (heaven help us) even greater things.[15] In spite of that high calling, we often organize and orient our communities, congregations, and denominations, toward less nebulous, less challenging ends. But the operative word there is *less*. We regularly submit ourselves to the ways and means of the consumerism of our time. Nothing can be too hard, or too strange, or too demanding. We often spend more time working on our budgets than praying for discernment. We draft mission statements meant to appeal broadly, but which are sufficiently vague that they don't scare anyone off. We reduce our expectations on members to showing up monthly if it fits in their schedules. We often spend vastly more time and energy on bureaucracy than on discipleship. We take our leadership models from the business world. All of these things could be viewed in a more positive light than I am suggesting: bureaucracy can be helpful, grace for the overextended is good, stewardship matters, leadership is important. But as often as not, the church tends to look rather more like the world around us than an alternative possibility.

---

13. The situation is sometimes different in the United States, the culture we most closely mirror. But the majority of my American Christian friends would likely express similar doubts, the current right-wing entanglements notwithstanding.

14. Col 1:16.

15. John 14:12.

I recall laughing at the fact that a previous edition of the United Church of Canada Manual, the resource for denominational polity, commissioned the elders (or Session) of the local church to take responsibility for congregational discipline. Not the praying and fasting kind of discipline; the holding people to account in some meaningful way kind of discipline. In my tradition, that's increasingly hard to imagine. Even laughable. Try telling someone they need to shape up spiritually or morally, or question their parenting decisions or their marriage, and see how long they hang around anymore. Our consumerist, "have it your way" culture can't abide that kind of authority. Incidentally, the newest version of the manual says nothing about "church discipline." We seem to have given up on the notion that the Christian community might have something of value to say about how I live *my* life, which puts us in danger of mirroring the kind of community we would create if we were in charge.

But the church is not meant to look like we're running the show, getting after what we want. We're to be an icon for the world God wants. A community through which the world can catch a glimpse of what the living God is up to. We're to be like Jesus, even when his will and way confound our expectations and undermine our misplaced desires, as they often do. The most obvious evidence that we're meant for something else is that, for followers of Jesus, the way of life that is truly life is the way of the cross. The church is to be a cruciform people, which will put us at odds with the keepers of the way things are. Crucifixion was the way by which the Roman Empire punished rebels, which is to say, anyone who acted in a way contrary to the Roman will and way. Crosses were reserved for dissidents and troublemakers, disturbers of the *Pax Romana*—the Roman version of peace that was accomplished by killing anyone who opposed it. We follow the One who calls us to pick up our own crosses and follow him to his: to pick up our crosses is to willingly put ourselves at odds with the default assumptions of the culture that surrounds us.

In the more left-leaning parts of the body like the one that I spend most of my time in, we've often shied away from cross language. Even more from anything that sounds like substitutionary atonement, the belief that Jesus died for *my* sins and ours. The more "seeker-sensitive" a church is, the less likely you are to see a cross anywhere. The cross is a threat to our ability to self-satisfy spiritually, and the cross confronts the lie that we're going to fix the world if we can just get our acts together. The cross is an affront to our best will and efforts; it's not really a consumer option. The cross lays bare the true paucity of our privileged imagination that the world depends on us. The cross is the stark reminder that we are saved by grace and grace alone.

I confess my own discomfort with certain versions of substitutionary atonement that say that God simply executed an innocent person instead of the rest of us. But the discomfort tends to evaporate in the company of the Trinity. The death of Jesus is not the sacrifice of the Son to appease a bloodthirsty and wrathful Father, it's the refusal of God, in Godself, to hold anything back for the sake of the world. It's God keeping God's promises to this beloved creation, even if it kills him. That God loves us is not self-evident, and it can only be imagined to be self-evident when everything is going more or less well. The way that we know the full height and depth, the length and width of God's love is in the person of Jesus: his life and death, his resurrection and reign.

When we set aside our privilege and crawl out from under the crushing weight of self-assurance, when we unbind ourselves from the fear of vulnerability and shuffle to the foot of the cross, we find ourselves in the presence of the One who will not be anything but with us and for us, whether we deserve it or not. We find ourselves in the presence of the God who is familiar not just with our delights but with our sorrows, not only with our victories but also with our defeats. The cross reveals the God who won't cut and run when things get difficult and worse, the God to whom we can draw near alongside the downtrodden and the broken, even covered in the dust and ash of our best-laid plans. The cross is why we can pray with Christians in a bombed-out Ukrainian church, or the opioid-devastated Downtown Eastside of Vancouver, or sing with those Christians around the world who risk their lives to worship, or continue to be people of creative peace when all is destruction and violence. The cross is why we can give ourselves over to an alternative possibility: a hope and peace and joy and love that isn't given in anything like the transactional ways that we're used to. It's why we can risk not just calling Jesus "Lord," but actually living like we believe it's true and doing what he says, because he did it first.[16]

James K. A. Smith likens following Jesus to a dance. Drawing from the writing of Clair Wills, he points to her insight that in a partner dance, there are actually two leaders—the leading dance partner and the music.[17] The church is called to follow the One who follows another—moving according

16. Luke 6:46.
17. Smith, *How to Inhabit Time*, 93–94.

to the rhythms of heaven's kingdom. Jesus never chooses his own rhythm, but lives and moves in perfect time with the Father's creative voice.[18] Those of us who would follow Jesus must attend to both the song that birthed creation, and him who leads us in step with that eternal tune. This means that learning the way of Jesus is not passive obedience, but active response. "[The dancer] must be relaxed enough to feel the slightest of cues from her partner, and yet sufficiently poised, mentally and physically, to be able to play—to respond, to hold back, to make form out of commitment, interruption and hesitation."[19]

In the Christian life there is more than the cross, but the cross must be at the center. It must shape us. It is the crescendo toward which heaven's love song was always building, and from which its beautiful resolution flows. We may prefer Easter Sunday to Good Friday. But without the cross, there is no resurrection in which to find our hope. *And there is resurrection.* To talk of the cross, of being cruciform, is not to suggest that Christians should be a self-flagellating, joyless, and severe people. Not at all. In fact, our resurrection hope should mean that we are a people prone to rejoicing.

We rejoice because in Christ we have seen the promise that the things that tempt and deform us have no real power. The sin that clings and binds will not hold forever; the way things are is not the way that they will be. Instead, the Way of Jesus puts us in cahoots with the God who delights in new creation. We rejoice because we have seen in Jesus that his way of *humility, self-giving, and steadfast faith* is the will and way of God for us and all things. The cross shows us the lengths to which God will go to love the world into newness and wholeness; the resurrection is the promise that divine love, and nothing less, will be ours right to the end and then through it. That's what allows us to dance the dance of Jesus 'til they crucify us, knowing that we'll rise to dance some more.[20]

Humility

Humility is our natural posture in the presence of God. In part, because with God we recognize that we are dealing with the One whose ways and thoughts are "high above" ours.[21] With the God of Israel and the church we

---

18. John 5:19–23.
19. Smith, *How to Inhabit Time*, 94.
20. Claiborne, *Irresistible Revolution*, 232.
21. Isa 55:8–9.

aren't dealing with a peer, or a slightly better projection of ourselves; we're drawing near to the One whose glory thunders and whose presence shakes the wilderness.[22] We are out of our depths when it comes to God. But the remarkable claim of both Israel and the church is that this God is also the One who welcomes us, and the One in whose presence we are made glad. To know this God, to feel the welcome of this God, is to know that we would gladly be servants in his household, just to be nearby.[23] Here humility is a position of gratitude and joy.

A church learning and formed in the Way of Jesus—the rhythms of grace and mercy, the pure gift of life in the presence of the Giver—will be a community marked by humility. We're called and claimed by the One who came not to be served, but to serve; the One who knelt and washed his disciples' dusty feet; the One who refused to grasp at power that was rightfully his and instead emptied himself for love's sake. It is impossible to walk the narrow path of Jesus if we're clamoring after power or grasping at control.[24]

Again and again, Jesus told his followers that the first would be last, and the last first in the kingdom of God. In the gospel of Luke we overhear Mary's song, which imagines a day when the lowly are lifted up, and the powerful in this world cast down.[25] Jesus told his disciples that they were to be childlike: to pursue the things of God with the curiosity, playfulness, wonder, and vulnerability of kids—a stark contrast to the armed soldiers representing Rome's interests, with whom they would have been all too familiar. St. James instructs the wealthy and powerful in his congregations to rejoice in downward mobility, and the poor to delight in their elevated status according to kingdom metrics. St. Paul has the audacity to tell his congregations to "regard others as better than yourselves," which was every bit as offensive then as it sounds now.[26] And he said that because it's the sort of thing Jesus would say. Because it's the sort of thing Jesus would do and does. From the get-go, followers of Jesus assumed that their community would look markedly different than the world around.

---

22. Ps 29.
23. Ps 84:10.
24. Matt 20:28; Mark 10:45; John 13:1–7; Phil 2:5–11.
25. Luke 1:46–55.
26. Phil 2:3.

Humility is the peculiar and proper posture of the church, and a defining characteristic of how we live and move and have our being in the wider world. The implications are social and theological.[27]

Socially, humility is meant to be embodied in the ways that we are with each other within the church—learning to see one another no longer from a human point of view, but as God sees them in Christ; growing in grace and mercy toward one another; bearing each other's burdens; rejoicing with those who rejoice; daring to think more highly of others than ourselves, not masochistically, but delighting in the beloved creature before us; taking the example of our Lord who knelt down and washed the feet of his disciples, even his betrayer's. And it is embodied in acts of service and generosity toward those outside our communities; caring for the least and the lost, giving of our resources for the flourishing of others, even when they can offer us nothing in return.

Theologically, the strongest case for a default to humility is a robust doctrine of the Trinity. Christians affirm that we know God to be one God, Father, Son, and Holy Spirit.[28] Scripture shows us the Father pointing to the Son, the Son revealing the Father, and the Spirit making both Father and Son known, while both Father and Son entrust themselves to the witness of the Spirit. There is mutual and loving submission flowing from the very being of God. The doctrine of the Trinity helps us understand that God's glory is paradoxically rooted in God's willful vulnerability, and passionate mutuality, which allows us to imagine something similar for ourselves, created in God's image.[29]

The Trinity helps us recognize that God's way, and hence the Way of Jesus, is essentially communal, rather than individualistic or dictatorial. The singer-songwriter, Steve Bell, puts it well: "I believe it with all my heart, that God is a unity of persons, and this unity, mutuality, and love has always been. If God were a uni-person, God could not be love, only will, and hence the primary action of God would be power not love. If God were a personality-less benevolent energy, all particularity, distance, distinction, and ultimately all individual consciousness would eventually cease or at

---

27. Our theology and our living are never separable. They're mutually revealing. How we live says more about what we believe than what we say; and learning to think well about God necessarily changes how we live. Nevertheless, for the moment, we'll think about them separately.

28. Fully unpacking the doctrine of the Trinity is well beyond the scope of this work. For a helpful introduction, see Byassee, *Trinity*, and, Myers, *Apostles' Creed*.

29. Gen 1:27.

best be meaningless."³⁰ As persons created in the image of the Person(s) we neither default to a hierarchy that values some over others, nor do we lose ourselves in mindless submission.³¹ Instead, we're made, in love, to strive constantly for the flourishing of one another.

One more theological consideration, which leads us to how we are meant to live not just within our particular communities but in the wider world, is that the communal confession of God as Trinity should keep us from insisting that one way or church tradition has the first and final say on who and how God is. The very fact that anyone who has ever tried to explain the Trinity knows how next-to-impossible it is, should keep us theologically humble. Our goal should be communion with God, not getting God right.

It is telling that, when confronted by Jesus after he's raised from the dead, the disciples' first response is terror and doubt. Would that it were otherwise, but that seems about right, humanly speaking. Even when they shift, ever so slightly, from terrified doubt, it is a peculiar comfort to know that they only make the leap to disbelieving joy.³² The Scriptures' honesty about these things is an act of holy generosity. It may be that what Christians are to be about should always be tinged with a hint of doubt and disbelief, a touch of terrified joy. When it comes to God, we're never treading on uncertain terrain—it is solid ground, sure, but it's ground over which we're being led, childlike; it's not a territory that we master.

The disciples' response to the risen Jesus tells us that our witness is always to something not perfectly graspable. The church is a much more interesting crew when we're pointing at something that won't be tamed by appealing to common sense or pinned down by rigid dogma and inflexible doctrine. Our witness is, as often as not, like the one who shrugs his shoulders and says, "Jesus, I don't quite get; what I do know is that I was

---

30. Bell, "Symphony and Trinity," para. 11.

31. The theological language of "Persons" of the Trinity is both helpful and challenging. It allows us to name, address, and engage the individual members of the Godhead, but risks "making God subservient to a human metric or projection, rather than the incomprehensible God who is ultimately known in the humanity of Jesus Christ." In other words, it's important to remember that when we speak of the personhood of God, "we reflect God, God does not reflect us." Likewise, the image of God as Father should not be taken as a reflection of human masculinity (in whatever form that takes), but a relational metaphor. Bennett and Moyse, "Learning Personhood Again," 10, 12.

32. Luke 24:37–41.

blind and now I see."[33] This is not to suggest that we can't say anything with confidence; we're not left with only questions and vagueness. But we say what we say knowing that our language and understanding will always fall short of the fullness and glory of God. What's more, there are significant benefits to theological humility. For instance, it can help us seek unity and cooperation with other parts of the body, perhaps some with whom we're not thrilled to be connected.

We do well to remember that the life of the church kicks into high gear at Pentecost, when the Holy Spirit is poured out. The story goes that the disciples were spontaneously, *pneumatically* able to speak in every language under the sun—or at least as many as Luke, the author of Acts, could name.[34] The point here is that the gospel can't be expressed in only one language, understood best by its native speakers. The gospel demands to be translated, spoken intimately. This implies that a full gospel expression requires the witness of an unnerving multiplicity of cultures. Again, the good news of Jesus Christ both transcends and takes shape within every culture.[35] We cannot assume that our preferred and most comfortable expression of God's presence and action in the world is the only one.[36] God wants the world, not just our church. In the end, all the nations of the world—every people, tongue, and culture—will bring their glory to the heavenly banquet.[37]

A spirit of theological humility allows us to move not just within the complex body of the church. Such a posture helps us move through the whole world in faithfulness, and with eyes wide open for the God who makes a habit of doing the unexpected, with the unexpected. It allows us to live out a core conviction of the gospel, that God was, in Christ, reconciling *all things* to himself through the blood of the cross.[38]

---

33. John 9:25.

34. Acts 2:1–12.

35. Jennings, *Acts*, 8, 17.

36. Of course, not every expression of Christianity is going to be equally faithful. We need not accept that those with whom we disagree are nevertheless "right." But neither are they usually totally wrong. For instance, I disagree with my fundamentalist friends when it comes to biblical interpretation. But goodness we mainliners could learn something from the seriousness with which they want to take the God who makes the mountains tremble.

37. Rev 21.

38. Col 1:21, italics added.

That's the sort of bold claims the church is meant to make about the way things are. We're a people learning to live in the hope that the life, death, resurrection, and reign of Jesus is the hope of the world and the foundation all reality. The person and work of Jesus is not just instructive for our individual living; he's the fullest expression of what it means to be alive in the world. He's how God is. What we know of truth, we know through him. Orthodox Christianity—even generously orthodox Christianity—does not say that Jesus is one religious option among many, but that *he is Lord*, the name above all names.[39]

That's the truly good news—that how Jesus is, is how God is: relentlessly with us and for us, passionately committed to setting captives free and raising the dead, to a world made whole and new. In Jesus we meet the God who is working toward that day when we will gather along the banks of the River of Life, together under the Tree of Life that bears its fruit in every season, and whose leaves are for the healing of the nations. The church is bold to claim that future is already invading the present, drawing us toward itself. Why do we in the mainline want to relativize that promise? Why hold back?

Of course, I can think of a number of reasons: we couch our beliefs because we want to care about our neighbors of other faiths and no faith;[40] we don't want to be lumped in with the sorts of Christians who so often make the news not for their love but for their intolerance and vitriol. We're anxious about making claims about things we don't fully understand. We

---

39. Phil 2:11. Obviously, there are people in the church who would disagree with this statement—lots of them in my own denomination. But I want to contend that it is still the best news we've got, and importantly, the point is that it's Jesus who is Lord; not our opinions, theologies, or experiences, but Jesus himself. While that is in one sense an exclusive claim, if the writer of Colossians, or the Philippians hymn, or even the end of Revelation is right, then it is also the most inclusive claim we can make. If God is truly reconciling *all things* through Christ, that Christ will have his way is the most hopeful thing we can say.

40. It's worth acknowledging that the hesitancy and timidity, or simply outright relativism, with which we liberal Christians often approach interreligious dialogue is generally unhelpful. The easy implication that we're all basically saying the same thing, and serious disagreement should be avoided for the sake of inclusion, is a violence not just to our own beliefs but the beliefs of those with whom we are in conversation. While there is often overlap, and certainly we could learn from people who believe and live differently than us, some of the best of what we have to offer directly contradicts the claims of other religions. Interestingly, we rarely seem to expect our neighbors of other faiths to bend on their beliefs.

don't want to look weird or silly or feel the disdain of religion's cultured despisers.

That said, disciples of Jesus have always been making and living out these bold claims in and for a world that does not accept them. Here, St. Peter's instruction is helpful and needed: "Always be ready to make your defense to anyone who demands from you an accounting for the hope that is in you; yet do it with gentleness and reverence."[41] This instruction tells at least a couple of things about what it means to bear Christian witness in the world.

First, we're meant to be living in such a way that someone might think to ask us about it. Our lives are meant to bear the marks of the hope that is ours. There is assuredly room to discern what that looks like. But if our lives are looking more and more like Jesus, if we're doing the sorts of things he does without reservation, folks are going to wonder about it. Peter's instruction assumes that Christians are not living shyly about their convictions. It assumes that we're taking the bold claims of the gospel seriously.

Second, our witness—lived and spoken—is meant to be gentle and reverent. Many people in my tradition are wary of evangelism because we have in our minds a caricature that is neither gentle nor reverent. We picture angry street preachers condemning passersby through a bullhorn. (It's hard to be gentle while yelling into a bullhorn.) Or we think of tracts, meant to scare us into mumbling the Sinner's Prayer. Or the relentless badgering of the neighbor who can't get through a conversation without questioning whether our name is as clearly written in God's good books as theirs is.

What would it look like instead to bear confident, bold witness to the will and Way of Jesus, gently and with reverence? Surely, that would require humility. It would mean taking seriously the fact that we cannot know what God is doing in and through another person. It would require us to take others with divine seriousness, as those whom God loves passionately and without reservation. Our witness cannot be marked by reverence, if we never pause to consider the person in front of us; if we refuse to count their story as bound up in God's love story with the world, even if their narrative is different than ours.

This doesn't have to devolve into relativism, the idea that one held truth is as good as another. As often as not, relativism ends up taking nobody seriously, under the guise of taking everybody seriously. Or, we pick and choose what suits us like the well-trained consumers that we are. To

---

41. 1 Pet 3:15.

suggest that one understanding of the world is as sound or good as another, or to take from others piecemeal, is an act of violence, not gentleness or reverence. Jesus was both "gentle and humble in heart," and perfectly willing to call people to account, to stand in the way of oppression and abuse, to side with the weary and heavy-burdened.[42] But if we begin with a posture of humility we may well find that we hear something we would not have heard; that we catch a glimpse of God's grace that either force or indifference would miss; that we learned something of God that we could not have known, except that we tended to the *imago Dei* in front of us.

Gentleness and reverence, borne of a spirit of humility, reminds us that we bear God's image, God doesn't bear ours. Gentleness and reverence help us understand that the gospel call to repentance is not for some, but for all. They help us come to terms with the fact that Jesus could happily call a tax collector and a zealot—a sell-out to the Romans alongside a Jewish insurgent—to be his disciples, and expect that they would both be changed, transformed for something greater.[43] Gentleness and reverence can help us avoid submitting to idols, and learn to live as icons of God's dream for the world.

It's worth acknowledging, before moving on, that I live out of a place of privilege, in just about every way. Downward mobility is something I actually have to work at. My assumption in all of this is that the church is tasked with harboring the vulnerable, not harming them; that our special concern, like Jesus's, must be for the weary and heavy-laden. That's what "religion that is pure and undefiled" looks like.[44] The call to humility—the task of being a cruciform people—should never become a limited call that keeps some people submissive, or condemned, while others wield power and authority. The call to humility is a call to be relentlessly concerned for the flourishing of each other, all of us under the Lordship of the One who came that we might have life and have it abundantly.[45]

Self-giving

Self-giving and humility, in the Way of Jesus, go hand-in-hand. A community growing in the way of the One who is sung in the law, the prophets, and

42. Matt 11:28–29.
43. Matt the tax collector (also called Levi), and Simon the Zealot.
44. Jas 1:27.
45. John 10:10.

the psalms is going to be one that forgoes individualism and self-concern, for the sake of communal well-being. Rabbi Laura Duhan-Kaplan puts it well: "Under biblical law, no one has any rights. No one can claim anything from the community. That's just not the language biblical law uses. Instead, everyone has obligations toward others, because that's how community is built."[46] The prophets regularly resound with such a spirit of generosity, and decry those who work for self-protection, rather than self-giving—especially at the expense of the vulnerable. Often, they point to a future time, when all creatures will live for the sake of mutual flourishing.

In the wake of Jesus's death, resurrection, and ascension, the church believes that God's future time now overlaps with our present. What *will be*—the world as God wants it—has invaded what *is*. Obviously, we're awaiting the fulfillment of God's dream for the world, but in Jesus, we've caught such a marvelous glimpse that we can't help but trust that not only is that day on its way, but it's already begun. The church is made to be the "first fruits" of the harvest we're hoping for.[47] So, in Acts 2 and 4 we see the nascent church living out a radical material *and* spiritual generosity that transformed the lives of those who embraced it—both those who gave and who received. It's a beautiful communal embodiment of the extravagant grace of God that has been experienced in the lives of those caught up in the wonder of resurrection. It testifies to the fact that what is experienced in Jesus must be expressed, and even more wonderfully can be.

In Acts 5, though, there's a harder story: here we meet a married couple, Ananias and Sapphira. They are a part of the early Jesus movement. They are caught up in the generosity of the community. Like others, they sell some property in order to share the proceeds with those who need it. Only, in contrast to another member, Barnabas,[48] who also sold a property and gave the money, Ananias and Sapphira decide together to keep a bit back. Their choice doesn't seem like a particularly devious thing. It might even have been rather pragmatic. They still sold the land and gave generously, which they did not have to do. Why not keep a bit, just in case? But, the story goes, Peter catches wind of what the couple had conspired to do, and he demands to know from Ananias "why has Satan filled your heart to lie to the Holy Spirit and to keep back part of the proceeds of the land?" The question lands so heavily that Ananias drops dead on the spot. A little

---

46. Duhan-Kaplan, *Mouth of the Donkey*, 23.
47. Jas 1:18; 1 Cor 15:23; 2 Thess 2:13.
48. Acts 4:36–37.

while later, not knowing what had happened, Sapphira shows up and more or less the same thing goes down. She claims that they gave all the money; Peter accuses her of conspiring against the Spirit of the Lord; the conviction crushes her and she dies.[49]

I've never liked this story. Peter can seem vindictive and even cruel. Though that could just be the tone I've given him. If we can hear in his voice the grief of a heartbroken brother who understands what's at stake, rather than a stern and uncompromising leader who is happy to see the disobedient struck down, the whole thing takes on a rather different quality. Even though we're told that it's the kind of thing that struck terror into the hearts of anyone who heard it, I don't think that fear is a great good news motivator. After all, perfect love casts out all fear.[50]

It is undoubtedly a story meant to make us know that the Holy Spirit doesn't deal in half-measures. But Willie James Jennings offers an insight that I think is worth attending to. He calls this story "The Death of the Sovereign Couple."[51] He pays special attention to the fact that Luke is careful to tell us that the choice to keep money back was a "conspiracy" between husband and wife, behind closed doors. They were elevating the concerns of their home life above the life of the community. Jennings contends that this is the Spirit's assault on our notion that there are places and spaces—specifically, in this case, the marital relationship—where the Lordship of Jesus is up for questioning. This reading makes perfect sense of my experience, both personally and communally. We have a tendency to imagine that decisions made in the privacy of our homes, married or not, supersede the needs and expectations of the community—that our private rights transcend our obligations to others. We do this all the time. *Caveat lector.*

Could we extend the challenge of Ananias and Sapphira to our church communities? I think it matters that the couple was, in significant ways, "in." They were committed to the cause, mostly. They sold property that they didn't have to sell and gave a significant (I'm assuming) portion of the proceeds to the life and work of the church. If Peter doesn't want Ananias and Sapphira, I'll gladly have them in any congregation I'm a part of!

Like the Sovereign Couple, as churchgoers we generally assume that we're "in," even if imperfectly. At least we're showing up, right? Lots of us are giving in ways that we have no social or cultural obligation to do so. But

---

49. Acts 5:1–11.
50. 1 John 4:18.
51. Jennings, *Acts*, 52.

I wonder if we ought to hear a kind of parabolic challenge to pay attention to the ways in which we conspire *as congregations*, either at the leadership level or as a whole, to hold a little back. You know, just in case.

When the future of our churches is not guaranteed, where the territory ahead is uncertain and even unstable, we are easily tempted toward self-protection. Ananias and Sapphira's decision makes sense to me. They're trying to balance prudence and faithfulness, security and generosity. But the Holy Spirit tends not to be about prudence or security or balance, at least not on our terms.

As a pastor, I am among the guiltiest when it comes to trying to manage the future. I have often held a little back, weighed options against budgets and other resources; I'd usually rather have a strategic plan than submit to the unpredictability of the Spirit. Of course, this kind of self-protection is the natural mode for people who have learned to believe that we are our own. That we are the first and final arbiter of what we ought to do. Maybe the hardest thing about the story of Ananias and Sapphira is that they remind us that we are not our own, and even less so is the church *ours*. The church does not belong to us, we belong to the church.[52] "You did not choose me," Jesus says to us and through us. "I chose, and appointed, you."[53]

It's a hard thing for a privileged people to hear. And yet, in the end, it is what claims and saves us. We're bold to say that our hope is in God's choice, not ours. As my colleague Sumarme Goble puts it, "God says 'I love you' first." And then God awaits our response. Praise God that's the order of things.

We need the gracious reminder that the church does not exist for itself. Yes, we are tasked with passing on the faith and practice that shape us in the way of Christ. So, we care about the future of the church. But we are, as has been often said, an organization that exists principally for its nonmembers. The church is meant to be an icon of God's dream *for* the world. The church doesn't exist as an end in itself; we're not called together, built living stone upon living stone either for ourselves simply for our own spiritual well-being or to draw people to ourselves and get people to join "our" church.[54] Ours is the God who pours himself out completely, for love's sake. We exist to do the same, in, with, and for this God-beloved world.

---

52. Jennings, *Acts*, 54.
53. John 15:16.
54. 1 Pet 2:4–12.

Faithful, Come What May

Mercifully, we're not asked to figure out what it means to be radically self-giving on our own. In fact, and perhaps obviously, it's almost impossible to be self-giving in isolation.[55] It's community that allows us to be faithful to the will and way of God in Christ, come what may.

Whether we consider the reality that we know God most fully as the community of the Trinity, or that God's decision from the get-go is creation-as-community, or that God's salvation mission begins with the choice of a people, or that Jesus himself had no illusions that his was a solo mission, it's abundantly clear that Christian faith and practice can't be individualistic. It's not just the obvious fact that for us to be self-giving, there needs to be another who is the object of our generosity, we also need to be in relationship with others who will seek our flourishing, as we seek theirs. We need people around us who can challenge us by their example, hold us accountable, and be bearers of God's grace when we falter.

It's always in the company of others that we learn to say what Jesus learned from his mom and she surely learned from her community: "let it be with me according to your word." Or, "not my will, but Yours." Or, again: "Your kingdom come, Your will be done; not ours." It's only in the company of others that we can have both the confidence and the boldness to not only say but to live these things. If we take Mary's song seriously, which she sings after she has committed to God's will and promise and which sets the stage for Luke's Gospel, it doesn't take long to understand that the things God is up to are likely to be disorienting at best.[56] There are not many people in most of the churches that I've spent my time in for whom it's not a mixed blessing when she sings about great gospel reversals like the high and mighty brought down and the lowly lifted up, the rich going hungry and the poor eating their fill, God's merciful commitment to a people who are peripheral by any worldly metric.

Most of the people I spend my time with, in and outside the church, fall on one side of Mary's ledger. For instance, by global standards, we are wildly rich. Forget the diabolically rich whose names come to mind. Even the poorest among us, more often than not, have access to a standard of

---

55. While there are certain monastic traditions that give the impression that isolation is the goal of their practice, even that is done with the understanding that the monastic's life of solitary prayer is done in service of the church, and by extension, the world.

56. Luke 1:38, 46–57.

living that many millions of people can't fathom. If the rich will be brought low, we can anticipate a change in position.

Frederick Buechner says that the gospel is usually bad news before it's good news.[57] When we realize that God is going to get the world God wants (good news!), we realize in fairly short order—if we're paying attention to the biblical witness—that the way things are is not the way that they will be (less good news, for most of us). Honesty should compel lots of us to acknowledge that "the way things are" has worked out pretty well for us. But as we learn to see the world through Jesus, to pray for God's kingdom instead of ours, we recognize that there will be gift in our downward mobility. We learn to trust that God's will is good, even when it contradicts our every instinct for self-preservation. A cruciform church is a community in which we learn to live and move and have our being according to different metrics than we've become accustomed to elsewhere. A cruciform church is a community in which we learn to say and to live, "Here I am, the servant of the Lord. Let it be with me according to your word." We learn more and more to do that, even when it costs us, come what may and even if we're counted as rebels in the world. To pick up our crosses is to choose a different way than the power brokers have sanctioned. In a world of bland submission to "the way things are," we are learning to live for the way that things will be.

The world needs a church ready and willing to sell out for an alternative possibility to the status quo. The world needs a church who knows in its bones that if Jesus is raised from the dead, nothing is the same. If Jesus is raised from the dead, and even more if he is ascended to heaven's throne, then that means that his will and way is God's will and way. In his name, we are called and claimed not by the spirit of our age, but by the Spirit of the Living God.

Imagine what it would look like if everyone of us who would check "Christian" on a census chose to commit ourselves to growing in the fruit of the Spirit: love, joy, peace, patience, kindness, generosity, faithfulness, gentleness, and self-control.[58] Imagine the ripple effects of churches relentlessly pursuing these things, no matter the cost. I think we would find ourselves more alive than ever, caught up in more than we would ask or imagine, and eager to participate in a kind of downward mobility that would turn the world on its head. Or, more likely, put it back on its feet.

57. Buechner, *Telling the Truth*, 7.
58. Gal 5:22–23.

Part of the challenge for every church, in every generation, is that Jesus reminds us that when God's will takes shape it's never a vague generality. Our gospel ideas must become tangible; the Word always becomes flesh.[59] It's easy to speak broadly and limply about love, joy, peace, and so on, but when we pray that God's kingdom would come on earth as in heaven we commit ourselves to something practical and particular. We don't love generally. We don't experience joy as a vague ideal. We don't pursue peace in abstract. We do these things with our feet on the ground, with and for the people in front of us, in the time and place we find ourselves. Doing so takes commitment, even when it's hard. It will not be accomplished by a few visioning meetings, or a solid strategic plan, helpful as those things might be. Fortunately, churches are home to lots of "long-haulers," folks who have seen the ups and downs and stuck it out. And even more fortunately we're not on our own: it's the Spirit of the living God at work in us both to will and to work for God's good pleasure.[60]

Over the next two chapters we're going to look at how Jesus's resurrection framework, the Christ-shaped realities of repentance and forgiveness of sins, can help us discern what all this might look like, wherever and in whatever kind of church and context we find ourselves.

---

59. John 1:14.
60. Phil 2:13.

Chapter 3

Repentance

The time is fulfilled, and the kingdom of God has come near; repent and believe in the good news.

MARK 1:15

Repent, for the kingdom of heaven has come near.

MATTHEW 4:17

BOTH THE GOSPELS OF Matthew and Mark tell us that Jesus's first sermon, when he came Spirit-launched out of the wilderness and into his ministry, was a call to repentance.[1] Luke tells it a bit differently, saying simply that Jesus began to teach.[2] But Luke quickly moves to a scene in which we get to overhear one of Jesus's early sermons. He's in Nazareth, where he grew up. On the sabbath day he goes to synagogue, as he always does. He takes the scroll of the prophet Isaiah and reads:

> The Spirit of the Lord is upon me,
> because he has anointed me to bring good news to the poor.
> He has sent me to proclaim release to the captives
> and recovery of sight to the blind,

1. Matt 4:17; Mark 1:15.
2. Luke 4:15.

>   to let the oppressed go free,
>   to proclaim the year of the Lord's favor.[3]

Then, as he rolls up the scroll, he says to the gathered crowd: "Today this scripture has been fulfilled in your hearing."

We could spend a lot of time working out exactly what Jesus means by *the scripture has been fulfilled*. But when we put it alongside Matthew and Mark's testimony about the content of Jesus's primary kingdom message, it becomes clear that what Jesus is on about is a radically new political reality. Whatever the kingdom of God (or the kingdom of heaven) is, it's good news for those for whom good news has been in short order. It's freedom for those who are weighed down in all sorts of ways by the current order of things. It's a new economic reality: the "year of the Lord's favor" is the year of Jubilee, when debts are forgiven, and land is redistributed, which is to say, things are going to be different when God gets the world God wants.

When the kingdom of God comes near it's always in contrast to, if not conflict with, any other kingdom. Jesus doesn't call us to a slightly different way of being, he calls us to something altogether new. We shouldn't expect to only be comforted in Jesus's presence. There never was a Jesus "meek and mild." Matthew tells us that even as a baby Jesus struck fear in the hearts of those whose hope was in the world that they had made for themselves, and whose confidence was in their power to sustain "the way things are." We hear that King Herod was afraid when he heard the news of the birth of a rival king, and not just Herod but all Jerusalem with him.[4] The first thing Matthew wants us to know after Jesus is born is that his arrival signals a change in the order of things.

It's important to understand this political element as we think about what it means when Jesus commissions us to be witnesses of *repentance*. Repentance is more than feeling badly about some action or inaction. It's more than confession of sin. Confession is important for helping us recognize the things we have done and the things we have left undone that put us at odds with God's will and way, and acknowledge that we have fallen

---

3. Isa 61:1–2.

4. Matt 2:1–12. It's not clear why "all Jerusalem" were afraid. One possibility is that the people knew that a threatened Herod was almost certain to respond in violence, without concern for collateral damage. Another possibility is that the "all" here is really the Jerusalem establishment, the ones who matter, those privileged by proximity to the current king.

short of God's glory.⁵ Confession is important, but Jesus's goal and call is to repentance.

Repentance is a commitment to doing something qualitatively different. Repentance is the move from acknowledging when we fall short of God's glory, to moving toward and into that glory. For Christians, repentance is choosing to do whatever we do, in word or deed, in the name and Way of Jesus, to the glory of God.⁶ Which means that repentance is essentially, fundamentally, *political*.

It may set some of us on edge to mix church and politics, which is probably reasonable given the headlines; things have not always gone well when we've done so. As theologian Stanley Hauerwas puts it, "Mixing religion and politics is like mixing ice cream and manure. It doesn't affect the manure, but it sure affects the ice cream."⁷ For some, the answer to that is severing the political from the religious. Particularly in the mainline, we tend to be wary of churches where voting instructions are given from the pulpit. What's more, we're generally fairly pleased with ourselves that conservative and liberal voters might sit side-by-side in our pews. And perhaps, sometimes, we should be.⁸

One of the challenges of understanding the political aspects of Scripture is that for those who wrote and first read them, there was no separation between politics and religion.⁹ They were entirely intertwined, creating a coherent cultural understanding, rooted in the conviction that one part of life cannot be separated from another. In many ways, that is a much saner view of the way we are meant to live in the world. The disintegration of modern life, wherein what we do in one space need not have any connection to what we do in another, is an irrational and ultimately dehumanizing way to live. We're not made to be fractured; we're to be whole as God, in whose image we are made, is whole.¹⁰

---

5. Rom 3:23.

6. Col 3:17.

7. I heard him say this in a lecture given at the Vancouver School of Theology, in 2020.

8. Melissa Florer-Bixler argues convincingly that this satisfaction can only go so far in the church. If we are following Jesus, there will come a time, especially in matters of justice, when it's insufficient to be satisfied with the kind of relativism that often masquerades as tolerance. She makes clear that it is almost always the persecuted or less powerful who bear the burden of communal tolerance. Florer-Bixler, *How to Have an Enemy*.

9. Rowe, *World Upside Down*, 4.

10. Matt 5:48.

In the church, the problem with separating the religious from the political is that we are largely stripped of any capacity to make a claim on each other's lives outside of Sunday morning. (And sometimes not even then.) This is in part a concession to our secular age's insistence that God and culture are not dealing in the same currency.[11] Faith is private and doesn't have a place in the "public world" of politics. If we accept that, it follows that the rules that apply in church don't hold in any other sphere of our lives. But, even if we can come to the communion table with someone with whom we fundamentally disagree, what difference does that make if, once we've returned to our seats—and even more once we've left the building—we are not in some way challenged and changed for the sake of the other? And more to the point, what difference does it make if we are not each being shaped in the likeness of the One who gathered us together in the first place?[12] It's worth remembering that when Jesus calls us, it's through a narrow gate, not a multilane highway.

We know that Jesus was not opposed to calling folks who were diametrically opposed to one another into his movement. His closest disciples included Matthew the tax collector, and Simon the Zealot. As a tax collector, Matthew was in cahoots with the occupying Romans, grifting his neighbors in service of the empire. Whether Simon formally belonged to the revolutionary sect of the Zealots or not, the nickname suggests that he was awfully sympathetic to those who would vanquish the Romans by any means necessary. Jesus called both men and made them frontline ambassadors of something altogether different than either empire or revolt. His call put them both at odds with their own political inclinations. "You do you" is not a Christian option.

In the end, the question is not, "Is the church political, or should we be?" The question is, "How are we political?"[13] We can't help being political, humans are political beings, organizing ourselves in particular ways, to particular ends—or at least, stated ends. So, the church must ask ourselves not whether we are liberal or conservative or somewhere else on the political spectrum, but: do our politics line up with the ways and means of the kingdom of God?

---

11. Taylor, *Secular Age*, 15.
12. Florer-Bixler, *How to Have an Enemy*, 145.
13. Claiborne and Haw, *Jesus for President*, 235.

The Politics of Repentance

The Greek word *metanoia* means to rethink or, even more evocatively, to come out of our minds.[14] To be people of repentance is to be a people prepared to rethink what we think we know about the world, to come out of familiar mindsets, and exchange those established thoughts and patterns wholeheartedly for the ways of another. To be a people of repentance is to allow every aspect of our lives to be challenged, shaped, and healed by the will and Way of Jesus. And that is an essentially political act.

N. T. Wright helps us recognize the political nature of repentance. He considers a passage from the autobiography of the first-century historian and politician, Josephus. He tells of an incident, around 66 AD, early in the life of the church, not long after Jesus's ministry, as the New Testament was beginning to take shape, in which he went with official authority to Galilee to quell a brewing rebellion. While on this mission, an outlaw leader made a plot against Josephus's life. Josephus managed to foil it, and subsequently tells the rebel that he knew about the plot, but that "I would, nevertheless, condone his actions if he would show repentance and prove his loyalty to me."[15]

Wright continues: "'If he would show repentance and prove his loyalty to me.' The translation is accurate enough, but could just as well have been rendered, 'if he would *repent and believe in me.*' Josephus is requiring of [the brigand] that he give up his brigandage, and trust him (Josephus) for a better way forward."[16] Wright's point is that if this is how the language of repentance was used and understood in Galilee, in the middle of the first century, it is a reasonable assumption that it meant something similar in the twenties and thirties, when Jesus was preaching.[17] It likely would have resonated that way for the first gospel readers.

Repentance, in this context, was not about simply an interior change of heart or a willingness to admit wrong. In the time and place that Jesus preached repentance in preparation for the kingdom of God, it meant a practical, embodied willingness to trade one way of being for another.

---

14. It's a compound word: *meta*—over, against, and *nous*—mind. I'm grateful to Tim Keel for this insight.
15. Wright, *Jesus and the Victory of God*, 250.
16. Wright, *Jesus and the Victory of God*, 250.
17. Wright, *Jesus and the Victory of God*, 251.

> It was an *eschatological* call, not the summons of a moralistic reformer. And it was a *political* call, summoning Israel as a nation to abandon one set of agendas and embrace another. . . . This was not simply the "repentance" that any human being, any Jew, might use if, aware of sin, they decided to say sorry and make amends. It is the single great repentance which would characterize the true people of YHWH at the moment when their god [sic] became king.[18]

To repent is to live our day in, day out lives, as well as our life together, from the conviction that the will and way of God is the way things really are and will be. It's to start to live *now* our confidence that someday God's reign will be complete.

Jesus insisted, and Christians have come to believe, that how he is in the world is the clearest revelation of God's will, and what it will look like when the divine will holds full sway.[19] He is "the image of the invisible God,"[20] the One in whom the fullness of God dwelt among us, bodily.[21] He is the One whose ways and means make most fully known the ways and means of God.[22] To witness to repentance in his name is to proclaim and be claimed by *his* politics, in *his* way of being, for the world. We ought to pay attention to these prepositions. The poet-priest Malcolm Guite says that Christianity is not so much a propositional religion as a prepositional religion.[23] The prepositions matter. We are *in* Christ; we are *for* the world.

As we think about what it means to bear witness to repentance, in the name of Jesus, we cannot allow ourselves to imagine that whatever he's about is only for another time and place, somewhere, someday. The Word becomes flesh and moves into the neighborhood. What the church has to offer and what we're called to be has everything to do with this time, and this place—whenever, wherever we are. We are, to quote Rich Villodas, "Not a presence removed from this reality, but a presence that refuses to be shaped by it."[24] To bear witness to repentance is to refuse to be shaped by anything other or less than Jesus, whatever the cost.

---

18. Wright, *Jesus and the Victory of God*, 251.
19. John 10:30.
20. Col 1:15.
21. Col 2:9.
22. Heb 1:2–3.
23. Guite, *Waiting on the Word*, 88.
24. Rich Villodas, tweet, July 10, 2021.

Christ-shaped Politics

When it comes to talking Christian politics, it's worth remembering that the first thing Jesus does when he's raised from the dead, which is the inaugural act of God's kingdom, is open his disciples' minds to understand the Scriptures. Torah, the prophets, and the psalms tell us about the trajectory of God's politics.[25] Again, as Christians we read the Hebrew Scriptures through Jesus, interpreted and refracted through the witness of the New Testament.[26] This should lead us to the conclusion that we can't know the politics of Jesus outside the authority of Scripture. The only way to know what Jesus calls us to is by taking the Bible seriously. Otherwise, we may come up with perfectly coherent and convincing political platforms—on either side of the political spectrum—which will not, in the end, align us with the will and Way of Jesus.

Allowing ourselves to be shaped and challenged by the whole witness of God's people to God's action in and for the world requires our immersion in all of Scripture. It can be dangerous to isolate one passage or voice, as though they aren't in conversation with the rest. Still, if we want to talk about what it means to live lives of political allegiance to Jesus, it makes sense to start with the Sermon on the Mount.[27] This is Jesus's first major teaching, in Matthew's Gospel. It functions as his kingdom manifesto. It foreshadows that this is the sort of thing that his ministry will be about—and what he expects of those who want to join up. Which is really who this is for: folks who want in. From the start of the sermon it's clear that while Jesus's earlier call to repentance and kingdom readiness is for all who have

---

25. Luke 24:44.

26. One of the gifts of the Scriptures is that they are unabashedly self-critiquing. There are internal checks and balances that must be taken seriously. What's more, we naturally give more weight to some sections than others. I believe we're meant to. And I used the word "trajectory" of God's politics advisedly. I don't mean this in a supersessionist kind of way. I think that trajectory is baked into the pages of the OT. What we see, for instance, in Joshua doesn't line up terribly well with Isaiah's "peaceable kingdom." Ruth critiques the anti-Moabite sentiments in the books that precede her story. Job undermines the transactional blessings of Deuteronomy. YHWH's movement in the world is always toward justice, love, and righteousness. Christians believe we see that most clearly in the person and work of Jesus.

27. The Sermon is found in Matthew 5–7. Luke has a version of this teaching (6:17–49), but it's not quite as fleshed out. Also, I appreciate that I am mixing gospels, which may rub some more critical readers the wrong way. Nevertheless, I'm inclined to trust the wisdom of the church and think these witnesses belong together.

ears to hear it—everyone is welcome—it's also clear that his disciples are meant to be a peculiar kind of community.

The witness to repentance, political allegiance to the will and Way of Jesus, is not something to be imposed on the world. It's a particular undertaking, borne out in the lives of those who have committed to being like him, doing what he does—that is, to being his disciples. Disciples do what the master does. Disciples are apprentices. They imitate the teacher, they learn to move through the world like him, they represent him wherever they go. Matthew tells us that, as the sermon was brewing, Jesus moved away from the crowds, and his disciples came to him.[28]

This separation from the crowds doesn't mean that we should advocate for a kind of separatism—again, we're not ultimately removed from the world; we're just not shaped by it. And if we pay attention, what happens as Jesus teaches his disciples, as they are formed by his word, we see that the crowds can't help but come a little closer. The sermon begins with a movement away from the crowds, but it ends with the crowds eavesdropping in astonishment. Perhaps some are listening in disbelief, but it's a safe bet that some are captivated by what Jesus seems to think is possible among us. He says this stuff with an authority that turns heads. This points to the reality that when the church, the body of Christ, bears living witness to the stuff that Jesus calls us to, the world around pays attention. And folks tend to want in.[29]

So, what is it that Jesus seems to think is possible among us? What is it that captures imaginations and lights up hearts?

To begin, any collective of his disciples will be a community learning to believe that it's the poor and the pure, the peacemakers and persecuted, the mourners, meek, and merciful, those starving for righteousness, who are the truly blessed ones. These are the ones to whom the kingdom of heaven belongs. The Beatitudes (the list of "blesseds" that kicks off the sermon) explode our expectations of what a kingdom is about. Contrast what we read in the first eleven verses with what we see in any of the media that we consume. Try to imagine an advertising campaign for the Beatitudes. It's not likely to be successful.

And yet, this is what Jesus wants: a reorientation of his disciples' perceptions and expectations. From the get-go, he expects that his followers will refuse to be an idol of their culture's gods. Followers of Jesus are

---

28. Matt 5:1.
29. Acts 2:47.

expected to be an icon, a glimpse of a world in which every tear is wiped away and every hungry belly filled; we're to be a place where one can imagine Isaiah's peaceable kingdom as more than a pipe dream, more than a utopian fantasy.[30] We're to let it come alive in and among us. We're to be people of extravagant hope, not instant gratification. The Beatitudes demand that we ask ourselves whether our churches look like the kind of place that the kingdom of heaven blessed ones will gladly hang out. What does it mean to make space for such a possibility?

Jesus continues. He looks at his disciples, straight in the eyes, and says, "You are the salt of the earth, you are the light of the world" (verses 13–14). You *are* the ones called, commissioned, and equipped to live out God's dreams for the world. Not, you could be the salt of the earth and the light of the world if you were bigger, better, richer, smarter, better looking, or more faithful. You *are*. It's important to know what a wild thing this is that Jesus says. We're used to being told that we're great. Plenty of celebrities have made a career of telling us how wonderful we are, and just to "let our lights shine." Social media is littered with motivational quotes telling us to dig deep and be true to ourselves, as if it's obvious that everyone has this inner light that we're supposed to let loose. So, we might not think much of what Jesus says here. But it's hard to overstate how radical this is. No one thought this before Jesus said it.[31]

The folks to whom Jesus first said this would have had no framework for thinking of themselves this way, and even if they did, let's remember that the original disciples to whom Jesus says this were not religious all-stars. Most of them were so unremarkable that no one bothered to write anything down about them. The ones we do know something about tended to be fishermen and laborers, tax collectors and prostitutes. These folks came equipped with callouses and life lessons, not seminary degrees and titles. In other words, they were no better equipped than most people feel they are to be witnesses of God's righteous alternatives. But Jesus doesn't stumble over the words. There are no conditions in what he says. This ragtag gathering of nobodies and ne'er-do-wells with whom we are implicated is commissioned to "let *your* light shine before others, so that they may see your good works and give glory to your Father in heaven."[32]

---

30. Isa 11:1–9.
31. Rowe, *Christianity's Surprise*, 35.
32. Matt 5:16, italics added.

This will look like learning to be people who get after God's will in our lives and in the world with whatever we've got, wherever we find ourselves; who refuse the self-indulgent delights of anger; who decline to treat others as commodities for our satisfaction, but recognize them as the God-bearing miracles that they are; who make space for truth to be clear and bravely spoken; who seek after mercy; who, heaven help us, are learning to love our enemies and pray for our persecutors, even as we chase after justice; who are extravagantly, recklessly, generous.

Goodness. If nothing else, the sermon reminds us that Jesus loves us as we are, and too much to leave us that way, as the old saying goes. So it's little wonder that right at the heart of the Sermon on the Mount is prayer. This is where Matthew puts what we have come to know as the Lord's Prayer.[33] This is surely instructive. We see in all the gospels that Jesus's first disciples were as prone as any today to taking matters into their own hands. They had a knack for getting carried away by their own plans, their own hopes and expectations, which generally put them at odds with their rabbi—which is to say, put them at odds with who and how God is in the world.

Throughout the sermon, we could easily get the impression that following Jesus is mostly a matter of our best efforts. There's hardly a clause that can't be turned into some kind of holiness competition, or "works righteousness" strategy, a means by which we take our holiness into our own hands. The Lord's Prayer lands as a gracious relief. It's the promise that the primary work of being the church is not ours—it's God's.

While we live to let God's love and justice and righteousness take shape in our lives, the fulfillment of God's dream for the world is God's work. We don't force God's kingdom to come, we pray for it. We pray for provision from the One who provides for all creation.[34] We learn to forgive as we recognize our own need, and pray for our forgiveness; we're made gracious as we experience God's lavish grace. We recognize that there are "principalities and powers" working against us, opposing the world that

---

33. Luke's version can be found in Luke 11:1–4, as part of a longer teaching on prayer. This is a good reminder that there is plenty of artistic license taken in the writing of the gospels. The Sermon on the Mount is almost certainly not one teaching, but several stitched coherently and beautifully together. As Matthew begins his gospel witness, he invites us to pay attention to the fact that this will be the shape of Jesus's ministry. This is how he will move through the world, and the sort of radical reorientation he calls his disciples to.

34. Ps 104:14.

God wants, and we strive only in the resurrection hope that those powers will not get the last word.[35]

This prayerful interlude, in the midst of so many commands, teaches us that disciples of Jesus aren't simply running around changing the world. We're being changed for the world. Or, to paraphrase Robert Mulholland Jr., we're not meant to run ourselves ragged in the world for God; we're meant to be in God, for the world.[36] And the prayer that Jesus teaches at the heart of the sermon confirms that.

It's worth paying attention to the pronouns here, which are all plural. The wide expression of Christian spirituality throughout history teaches us that personal prayer and spiritual practices matter. And undoubtedly, our private lives matter to God. We get to cast our cares on the Lord because he cares for us.[37] We're called in intimacy, to know Jesus.[38] I'm a firm believer that God makes a claim on each of our lives, shaping divine will in the marvelous particularity that is each one of us. And, to state the obvious, I can't live out your baptismal vows for you, nor you for me.

But, as Jesus teaches us to pray, he makes plain that we do not—cannot—live Christianly on our own. This is not about less than "me and Jesus," but it's surely about more. The Lord's Prayer teaches us that—contrary to much popular belief—living in step with God's Spirit is not a solo venture.[39] In an "age of authenticity,"[40] when we are convinced that my individual spiritual journey and expression is my own and no one else's, Jesus teaches us to pray in the first-person *plural*.

As we try to figure out what it means to love enemies, or give generously, or what it means to walk through the narrow gate that leads to life, we do that discernment together. Salvation is a communal experience. The kingdom of heaven is not a gathering of isolated individuals; it's all creation, gathered in intimacy with God, in whose image we are created.[41] To

35. Eph 6:12.

36. Harris, "Mulholland."

37. 1 Pet 5:7.

38. Matt 7:23. Knowing, biblically speaking, is never just a matter of having the right information. It's a matter of intimacy. When Genesis tells us that Adam "knew" Eve (4:1), it's pretty obvious that this wasn't in the objective, scientific sense. When the Psalm invites us to be still and know that God is God (46:10) it's impossible to read that, let alone pray it, as a theological proposition. It's an invitation to intimacy.

39. Gal 5:16.

40. Root, *Faith Formation*, 3; Perrin, *Changing Shape*, 9; Taylor, *Secular Age*, 473.

41. Rev 22:3–5.

say that we are created in God's image is to recall that we are made to reflect the One who is triune—one God, three persons; perfect unity without loss of personhood.[42] Even when we pray on our own, behind closed doors, we join our voices with the great cloud of witnesses that surrounds us, whose prayers ascend to heaven's throne.[43] In a time when so many are experiencing deep, profound loneliness, the church is to be a place where we find ourselves knit together. We're a people who pray in plural.

A Colony of Heaven

Eugene Peterson writes that the church is made to be "a colony of heaven in the kingdom of death," which I have always found evocative.[44] Any colonial image needs to be used wisely, and if it can't be, then it should be discarded. It is used here in stark contrast to the ways that other kingdoms and empires have colonized the world. Where the colonizing practices of worldly powers tend to obliterate indigenous cultures in the name of the colonizers, the images appropriate to the kingdom of God are of flourishing, creative transformation, and intimate, self-giving love.

The heavenly vision is of all cultures marching joyfully into the city of God, neither losing their identity nor remaining static in it. To be a colony of heaven is not to impose an earthly culture—ecclesial or otherwise; it's to be a locus of transformation for the sake of the wholeness of everyone (human and nonhuman creature alike) that we come in contact with. Colonies of heaven assume that God is present and active before we show up. We're just looking to get in on what God is already doing. The point is that we're meant to be communities where the ways and means of heaven are being worked out in our lives—and through us, into the world. We're meant to be that light on a hill, bearing witness to fresh possibility. We're meant to be salt in a sin-bland world, bringing the flavors of heaven's feast.

The Sermon on the Mount ends with the reminder that we're not just supposed to be inspired or challenged or convicted by Jesus's words. We're supposed to live them, come what may. Maybe that's what had the crowds

---

42. The doctrine of the Trinity is one of the most important and complicated teachings of the church. It exerts a centripetal pull on all our other doctrines. Full treatment is beyond the scope of this project. For an accessible introduction to the Trinity, check out Byassee, *Trinity*.

43. Heb 12:1.

44. Peterson, *Practice Resurrection*, 12.

astonished in the end. These are not suggestions. They're not ideals. Jesus really does expect that what he teaches will find shape and expression in the lives of his disciples, wherever and whenever we find ourselves.

At the same time, it's not exactly plug and play, is it? What does it mean to "store up treasures in heaven"? Or to keep our eyes healthy? How do we make sense of Jesus's instructions not to worry about food, or drink, or clothing, or tomorrow and get after the kingdom instead? How do we discern what's good fruit, from the bad?[45]

To become doers and not merely hearers of these words requires more than a strategic plan.[46] We need to spend time in the sermon, meditating and praying through it, together and in private. The church should be a brave space to learn, even in "fear and trembling," to hold Jesus's words against our lives and pay attention to where they line up.[47] And when they don't line up, we count on God's grace, and we repent. We let God have God's way. We learn to trust that the foundation that Jesus is laying is surer than any we can come up with, and we begin to build our lives together on it.

How to live in faithful allegiance to the will and Way of Jesus, wherever we are and come what may, is a challenge that every generation of saints has faced and will face on this side of things. No matter where this word confronts us, no matter when, or with whom, its demands grate against the cultural assumptions of the surrounding world. There's a reason those first crowds were astonished: they understood that the kinds of things Jesus calls his disciples to put them on a collision course with the keepers of "the way things are." It's been so ever since.

But the communal nature of Jesus-shaped politics poses particular challenges for the church in the West, in the third decade of the twenty-first century. We live in a time and place of extreme polarization. The assumption that individual rights transcend any sense of a common good is rampant on both sides of the political spectrum. The generations coming into early adulthood have been shaped completely within the demands of what Charles Taylor calls "the Age of Authenticity," in which everyone is specifically and intrinsically responsible for their own beliefs, identity, and self-expression.[48]

45. Matt 6:20; 6:22–23; 6:25–34; 7:17.
46. Jas 1:22.
47. Phil 2:2.
48. Taylor, *Secular Age*, 473; Perrin, *Changing Shape*, 9.

This is not invariably negative by any means. There are significant advantages to not being limited by or restricted to cultural expectations, and there is obvious good in the ability and freedom of each person to choose a path that's not prescribed. That we need not do something simply because others assume that we should is a freedom that can allow for the kind of flourishing for which we are made. Of course, this means that for better and/or worse, the number of nominal Christians in the West is decreasing rapidly. Unlike other points in history, people must opt into Christian faith, in a way that was not necessary or even possible in the past. The "nones," those who claim no religious affiliation—either through indifference or hostility or wandering curiosity—is the fastest growing religious group in North America.[49] There is no good reason for someone to show up to church, except that we have something astonishing to offer.

This need not be all doom and gloom. In this post-Christendom world, the fact that cultural and generational Christianity can no longer be assumed presents some opportunities. I don't think we should rush to celebrate everything about the end of church as we have known it, but it does mean that we have every reason to dig in more deeply to Jesus's call to be a radical and beautiful alternative to the world around. That the church has a decreasing role in the systems that keep things the way they are means that we have an opportunity to explore the way that they *really* are—the way they will be when God gets the world God wants.

What's more, the overwhelming demands of "authenticity"—of determining and defining who I am, irrespective of, and indifferent to, any external pressure—has proven to be more burden than bliss. It's possible to celebrate the advantages while acknowledging that study after study shows that we are increasingly anxious and depressed, overwhelmed and disconnected, and that at the moment things are getting worse in each generation. Self-expression and self-exploration have turned out not to be as freeing or exciting as advertised.

The good news is that the *good news* has something to say about all this. Firstly, we can affirm without qualification that each of us is "fearfully and wonderfully made," uniquely gifted, each one a "living stone" necessary to building something extravagantly beautiful.[50] The biblical vision of creation is a world that teems with life, glorious in diversity. We insist that we're set free from whatever would bind and weigh us down, whatever

---

49. White, *Meet Generation Z*, 21.
50. Ps 139:14; 1 Pet 2:4–5.

keeps us from running fully and freely in the wide space of God's grace.[51] We're no longer subject to the demands and expectations of the culture around us—whatever that looks like—but in the life, death, resurrection, and reign of Jesus, God has worked out the conditions of our perfect freedom. And when the Son sets you free, you are free indeed.[52]

But secondly, Jesus doesn't set us free from everything and everyone. The biblical witness is that it's not good for us to be alone.[53] We're not meant for perfect autonomy. He sets us free for the purposes of living into our beloved creatureliness, for abundant life, for the sake of the world. We're free *for*, not just free *from*. Let's remember that the prepositions matter. As St. Paul puts it: "you were called to freedom, brothers and sisters; only do not use your freedom as an opportunity for self-indulgence, but through love become [servants of] one another." We are called and claimed by the One who didn't see his perfect, divine freedom as something to be clung to, but used that freedom to pour himself out in love, for us and for the renewal of all things.[54]

The good news for those of us who care about the future of the church, not just as an institution, but as a witness in the world, is that the generations in early and emerging adulthood are hungry for the freedom to be fully who they are, eager (though not always hopeful) for the renewal of all things, and desperate for intentional, mutually enlivening relationships. Pete Davis suggests that, "it's not just friends that people are craving. We're also craving the accountability that comes with being part of a mission-driven community."[55]

I am not suggesting that this all be packaged as a marketing campaign to get young folks back in church. But I do believe that, like every generation, we have everything we need to be the kinds of witnessing communities that will capture the imaginations of those within and without.[56] The church has been and can still be astonishing. There's a holy precedent for it. We can be the kinds of communities that move people from curiosity to commitment—commitment to one another, and more: commitment to the will and Way of Jesus in the world.

51. Ps 18:19.
52. John 8:36.
53. Gen 2:18.
54. Phil 2:1–11.
55. Davis, *Dedicated*, 38.
56. 2 Pet 1:3.

REPENTANCE

Of course, not everyone who walks through the doors of a church is looking to have their lives turned upside down—or right side up—by Jesus. And we should not be in the business of deciding what the Holy Spirit is up to in another's life. But there must be a core of people eager to go deeper, to really hear Jesus's words and do them, to prayerfully build their lives on a Christ-centered political platform. The excellent promise is that even two or three is plenty to get the party started.[57]

And it is, undoubtedly, much easier to write, preach, and say these things than to do them. I often think of the ubiquitous G. K. Chesterton quote that "the Christian ideal has not been tried and found wanting; it's been found difficult and left untried."[58]

The evidence is that many parts of the Western limb of the church have tried lots of other things that have been found wanting. But we should stop that. We have everything we need for faithfulness. We are the light of the world, not to be hid. We are the salt of the earth. We're not meant for bland obscurity. We're meant to bear witness to the repentance to which we are called. We're meant to let the future invade the present. We're meant to turn the world upside down.[59]

God give us grace and guts.

---

57. Matt 18:20. Chapter 5 will consider some practices that can help us live more fully into our call.

58. Chesterton, *What's Wrong With the World*, 37. I'm using his words slightly differently than he is—and we might disagree about some of what constitutes the Christian ideal.

59. Acts 17:6.

Chapter 4

Forgiveness of Sins

This forgiveness, articulated by Paul, is life together with the Son, sharing in his life and faith through the Spirit. This is the New place of life from which to live life in communion with God and the other saints.[1]

For as the heavens are high above the earth, so great is his steadfast love toward those who fear him; as far as the east is from the west, so far he removes our transgressions from us.

PSALM 103:11–12

MOST PEOPLE DON'T LIKE to talk about sin much. If we're churchgoers, our Sunday morning liturgies might require it of us. In my congregation every service begins, after an opening hymn, with a prayer of "approach and confession." Although I have heard of churches where confession is never entertained, lest someone feel badly about themselves, I think our church is not unusual. Most Christian communities are aware that everyone "sins and falls short of the glory of God."[2] And I expect that most mainline churches provide a way to acknowledge and deal with that fact.

Even so, while we don't mind making liturgical space for the opportunity to confess, sin is hard to talk about these days. It requires saying that something someone does or did is wrong in some way. In a culture where

---

1. Jennings, *Acts*, 230.
2. Rom 3:23.

each person is entirely responsible for being the first and final word on what is right and wrong for themselves, suggesting that something is off about someone else's behavior or decisions is likely to get us cancelled.

Adding to the challenge, if not the danger of talking about sin, is the fact that we live in a time and place when *what* we do is decidedly of less consequence than *how* we do it.[3] Being true to ourselves or being a good person—as we define "goodness"—is paramount. Our motivations and intentions are what really matter, and questioning these is off limits in most circumstances. What's more, in a wildly polarized culture, what's wrong for me might well be right for you, and that kind of tolerance holds no one accountable to anyone but themselves. For many, not conforming to any external expectations is the highest form of spirituality.[4] We are once more firmly rooted in a time when "all the people did what was right in their own eyes."[5]

Unfortunately, biblically speaking, the temptation to know right from wrong for ourselves is part of the primordial problem. Way back in the garden of Eden, the serpent's temptation wasn't riches, power, booze or sex—the things it's not polite to talk about in church. It was to be like God, with the ability to truly know right from wrong:

> Now the serpent was more crafty than any other wild animal that the LORD God had made. He said to the woman, "Did God say, 'You shall not eat from any tree in the garden'?" The woman said to the serpent, "We may eat of the fruit of the trees in the garden"; but God said, "You shall not eat of the fruit of the tree that is in the middle of the garden, nor shall you touch it, or you shall die." But the serpent said to the woman, "You will not die; for God knows that when you eat of it your eyes will be opened, and you will be like God, knowing good and evil."[6]

Looking more closely, the problem is not developing a moral compass, simply knowing right from wrong. Particularly in Genesis 2 there's incredible freedom granted to the humans to bring order and well-being to what God has made. They are meant to make decisions for the flourishing of the world. Humans are not God's puppets; we are God's image and agents, essentially engaged in God's good purposes for all things. Things go sideways

---

3. For more on this: Root, "End of Youth Ministry."
4. Root, *Pastor*, 17.
5. Judg 21:25.
6. Gen 3:1–5.

not with the desire to know right and wrong but to define it, to set the boundaries where we see fit. In other words, sin is the attempt to be as gods for ourselves. Fundamentally, the issue is not breaking God's rules, even if that is the visible action. Rule-breaking is symptomatic, not the sum total of sin. After all, following the rules can keep us out of trouble, but it can't change our hearts.

The issue is the humans' failure to understand who they are. They are not gods. *We* are not gods. We are not equipped for that gig. We are beloved creatures of the Creator, made a little lower than angels, made to participate with God in creation—not as gods for ourselves, but as the ones who bear God's image in the world. As creatures, we have a profound *priestly* vocation. We stand before God on behalf of all creation; we get to engage, tend, and nurture creation on behalf of God. But when we forget who we are—not gods, but creatures—our relationship with the One whose image we bear, and therefore our vocation in the world, is marred. Everything is skewed when we get that basic relationship wrong.

A Relationship Problem[7]

I have found that it's easiest and clearest in my context to talk about sin as a problem of distorted relationships. Genesis 3 shows us not simply the humans' failure to obey God's rules. Yes, the fruit is lovely, pleasing to the eye and good for food. But that's just the shape of the temptation. The juice dripping down the humans' chins is not, ultimately, the issue. Again, rules can keep us on the rails, but they can't capture our hearts.

What we see, the real devastation, is the unravelling of all relationships. We see this first in the choice to eat of the Tree of the Knowledge of Good and Evil—the one tree out of all trees that was to be off limits. The temptation isn't the fruit; it's to be as gods. That temptation is awfully seductive. We may not have a particular tree, but we are just as susceptible to trading the triune God for the trinity of our wants, feelings, and perceived needs.

The fallout of the Genesis decision shows us the consequences of our own self-idolatry. It's about more than overstepping a divinely imposed line. We're told that God came strolling through the garden, "at the time of the evening breeze." It's a marvelous image of intimacy, between God

---

7. In what follows, I am indebted to Leonard Sweet's keynote addresses at the Ministry in Motion conference, Wellington Square United Church, Burlington, Ontario, 2011.

and God's beloved creation. God is fully present to all that he has made. In the cool of the evening, God has come just to be with the humans. Simply to spend time with them. God wants their presence. But they're hiding in a bush. They are afraid of God. What was meant to be a relationship of intimacy and partnership has shriveled into fear. The humans' relationship with God is damaged.

They are not only afraid because of their disobedience. They're also afraid to be seen. They are racked with shame. They've realized that they are naked. Nakedness here is an image of perfect intimacy. Before this, we are told that the humans were naked before the Lord, and one another, and they were *unashamed*.[8] Nakedness is not meant to be a negative thing, but it's a symbol of perfect mutual vulnerability and trust, and the condition for new life to be made. But suddenly, that's not what the humans see. Now their vulnerability is a threat, not a gift. They make themselves pathetic leaf coverings, trying to hide their true selves. Shame has its way.

The humans' shame is a powerful image of our own distorted self-relationships. Without sin, there is no shame. Shame gets its claws into us and mangles what was meant to be good and beautiful, messing up our ability to see ourselves well. It causes us to hide ourselves, from God and each other. The human's first response to their sin is a cover-up. With whatever is at hand, they mask their nakedness. They do not want to be seen; they do not want to be vulnerable with one another; they do not want to be found by God.

Their quickness to cover themselves is also the first sign that the relationship between the humans is marred. Only a few verses ago, Adam couldn't contain his enthusiasm for Eve. You can hear the wonder as he recognizes that she is "bone of my bones and flesh of my flesh." But now their fig leaf loincloths are a symbol of division. Something has come between them. The breakdown of the interhuman relationship is capped off by Adam referring to Eve as "the woman whom you gave me." It's her fault, he insists. In that moment she ceases to be a gift of God: one who makes him burst into breathless love poetry, the partner who reveals something of God's goodness and grace, with whom the task of caring for the world is shared. Now she is a liability. Now he would have been better off without her. Now he blames her for his shame, for his disobedience, for his fear. It's easy to extrapolate, from his dismissiveness, disdain, and blame, the ways that our own relationships are distorted and diminished.

8. Gen 2.

I think it is important to see this as bearing witness to the breakdown in relationships between the sexes, but not only that. Certainly, I think Adam's response plants the seeds of misogyny that has thrived throughout history and continues to choke out life in our time and place, in our systems and structures and daily interactions. But this is also about broader interpersonal distortions. We need to remember that God made Eve principally so that Adam would not be alone, not just for sex or children. God can make people out of dirt. This is about more than procreation.

Moreover, when Genesis 1 tells us that God made humanity in God's image, both male and female, it's clear that God's image is borne not primarily in their union but integrally in themselves, as individuals. In both cases, the biblical authors are at pains to show us that every person, regardless of sex or gender, is meant to be both gift and icon of God. When we sin against one another we fail to receive and recognize the grace and glory inherent in every human life.

Finally, we see the relationship between the humans and the rest of creation begin to come apart, as Eve turns and blames the serpent for all of it. The humans are no longer bearing God's image for the sake of the created world; they are in conflict with the world. It becomes evident, as God outlines the consequences of the debacle, that the humans' experience of being in the world will be fraught. Genesis 3:23 is a powerful image of the disconnect between humanity and the rest of creation. We're told that "the LORD God sent [Adam] forth from the garden of Eden, to till the ground from which he was taken." We can feel something coming apart in that. Sin puts a kind of distance between us and the rest of God's good world. We work on it and over it, rather than in and with it. The capacity to understand and honor our connection to the earth, from which we are made, is warped.

At the time of this writing, the United Nations Intergovernmental Panel on Climate Change (IPCC) had just released its most recent report about the impending effects of human-induced climate change. It is well beyond sobering. The report makes it clear that we are a long way away from the vision of humanity as God's agents of care for this good and very good creation. As we, particularly *as Christians*, work to respond to the climate crisis, it's worth noting the telling fact that Genesis does not say that humanity is "good" in and of ourselves, unlike the other elements of creation. Our "goodness"—not morally but essentially—is integrally bound up with everything else. Our capacity to be fully and freely *what we are* has everything to do with playing our proper, God-given and God-revealing role in the ultimate wellness of all creation. All of creation groans, waiting for us to be remade in the holiness for which we are created.[9]

Witnesses of the Forgiveness of Sins

Taken as a whole, Genesis 3 shows us with poetic and prophetic imagination that, biblically speaking, sin is not simply a problem of behavior, but it's the breakdown and distortion of all the relationships for which we are properly made. This matters quite a lot when it comes to thinking about what it means to live out Jesus's commission to bear witness to the forgiveness of sins. It means, at very least, that our primary goal is not behavior modification, or "sin management,"[10] or removing all temptation and adhering perfectly to a prescribed way of being in the world. Our goal in the company of Jesus—both in terms of our work and our ultimate hope—is the reconciliation of all relationships: the relationship between us and God, within ourselves, between people, and with all nonhuman creation.

Rule-following does not get to the heart of the problem. Rules are necessary. Genesis testifies that good boundaries create the conditions for flourishing. But not coveting my neighbor's spouse, because I've been told not to, is not the same thing as taking my marriage seriously. Attending church out of obligation or fear is not the same as intimacy with God. Giving generously because the Bible says to is not evidence that we're eagerly seeking the flourishing of others or investing ourselves in God's reign. Naturally, not wishing I had someone else's spouse, or comparing mine to another's, gives me a better chance of being a good partner; showing up to weekly worship might well lead to a deeper experience of God's love and grace; developing patterns of generosity might make us more invested in the well-being of others. But simply doing these things does not guarantee fullness of life. We can be rigid in rule-following and lax in love.

We're not made for rules; we're made for right—that is, life-giving, life-nurturing—relationship, what we call "righteousness" in the church. Consider Paul's words to the Corinthian church:

> From now on, therefore, [in the wake of Christ's resurrection] we regard no one from a human point of view; even though we once

---

9. Rom 8:22.
10. Yaconelli, "Spirituality."

knew Christ from a human point of view, we know him no longer that way. So if anyone is in Christ, there is a new creation: everything old has passed away; see everything has become new! All this is from God, who reconciled us to himself through Christ, and has given us the ministry of reconciliation; that is, in Christ God was reconciling the world to himself, not counting their trespasses against them, and entrusting the message of reconciliation to us.[11]

The goal of a Christ-shaped community is not to get everyone to act a certain way. The goal of a Christ-shaped community is to join in God's work of reconciling the world. Paul's vision for the church is not a group of people behaving themselves—though we should not shy away from the fact that there are expectations for, and limits on, how we are called to live with one another as we grow up into the likeness of Christ. Paul's vision is the extravagant witness of a people living in profound intimacy with God, free from shame and distorted self-images, in love for one another, and toward the flourishing of all things.

Before we consider what that looks like, it is worth acknowledging that while the four kinds of relationship with which we are concerned can be considered separately for simplicity's sake (as they will be, below), they hold key things in common. Specifically, these relationships are inextricably connected, they are particular, and they are God-initiated.

One of the more common distortions of the gospel is that being in right relationship with God will have minimal effect on our everyday lives in the so-called secular world. We are told spiritual health is a private matter, and so we shouldn't get it too tangled with the dust and muck of the world. But Jesus makes clear that we can't love God well, without loving who and what God loves. As we think about what it means to join in God's ministry of reconciliation, it may make sense to focus specifically on one relational area or another. However, let's not imagine that we can address the distortions in one relationship without attending to the others. For instance, it's impossible to imagine what shame would look or feel like, outside our relationship to God and others. Shame is experienced personally, but its roots are communal and relational.

As well, we need to recognize the challenges and limitations of talking about these things generally. It's more than probable that the way I experience shame is not the way that you do. What I'm hiding of myself is not precisely what you are keeping hidden. My flimsy fig leaf isn't shaped like

---

11. 2 Cor 5:16–19.

yours. Still, I am confident that shame, in one form or another, is a universal experience, just as I am sure that everyone knows something about a disordered relationship with God, others, and the rest of creation.

As we try to imagine how our own communities can work toward a kingdom of heaven–style reconciliation, we need to bear in mind that the Holy Spirit has a tendency toward particularity. The Word becomes flesh and moves into the neighborhood. *Our* lives, *these* bodies, *this* community, *those* neighbors, *this* watershed all matter, not generally but specifically. The broad strokes that follow are just that. Our task as individuals and communities committed to the will and Way of Jesus in the world is prayerful, intentional discernment about how God is calling us to the ministry of reconciliation, not somewhere, someday, when we've got our acts together. But *where we are*, as we are, in *this* time.

Of course, not all our work will be limited to one place and people. But I would contend that it is easier than ever to support good initiatives elsewhere, than learn to love the people and places right in front of us. My monthly donation to a global nonprofit is a good thing, but it's easy compared to taking seriously the distortions and breakdowns in my own neighborhood, or even my own family. I'm still going to make the contribution to an important organization. But the fruit of the Spirit blossoms most lushly in the present and the particular.

Which leads to the most important point: we don't create the conditions for reconciliation. We enter the conditions that God, in Christ, has created. We begin by learning to trust that even now God is reconciling all things to Godself. A cruciform disposition is sustained by the expectation that God has acted and will act. It is easy to get caught up in our own projects, when God might well be calling us to do something else. As one old preacher put it, "If the devil can't get you to do something bad, he'll get you to do something almost good." We're not meant for "almost good," any more than we're meant for "pretty good news." Jesus came and called us that we might have life to the full, and he has sent us out to invite others into the same.

Four Relationships Restored

If the Genesis story shows us a world of unraveled relationships as a result of sin, then the forgiveness of sins must have to do with the restoration of those relationships. A community that proclaims forgiveness in Jesus's name will be one in which our relationships with God, ourselves, each other, and the whole nonhuman creation are being made new.

Our Relationship with God

The church's basic proclamation is that, in Christ, our relationship with God is restored. If we have been hanging around the church for a while, that may seem straightforward. But given the sheer quantity of books and sermons written over the past two thousand years about the nature of salvation, we should probably be humble and careful as we try to say just what it means that we are reconciled to God. Still, I believe that we must learn to say *something*. Our task as the body of Christ is to learn to give fulsome expression to the "new creation" conditions that God, in Christ, by the power of the Holy Spirit, is working in and among us.

In the church, we begin learning to speak our faith with the Bible, because the Scriptures put us in company and conversation with generation upon generation of people who have known the God we know most clearly in Jesus. The Bible reminds us that the God who made all things with a word can't be contained by our personal opinions and particular experiences. What we think, and the people, places, and events that have shaped those thoughts, matters: we get to love God with all our individual heart, soul, mind, and might. Because our God is a communal God—eternally Father, Son, and Spirit—we learn to love this God in community, which includes the communion of saints past and present. So, we tend to the Bible.

Though the Bible is a collection of diverse books and letters, poems and prayers, stories and strictures, written over hundreds of years and from many different places, Christians believe that the Bible tells a coherent story, in many voices, and that it testifies to God's ongoing action in and for the world. One thing that is clear in this story is that it begins and ends in intimacy: God is intimate and active in creation, and we are made in and for that intimacy.

In the beginning, we see this most clearly with the first humans. We see God present and personal, and God desires the peoples' presence. And at the end, in St. John's great vision of the world's future, we're shown that profound intimacy will be fully restored. As he experiences the world as it will be when God gets the world God wants, John sees

> no temple in the city, for its temple is the Lord God the Almighty and the Lamb. And the city has no need of sun or moon to shine

> on it, for the glory of God is its light, and its lamp is the Lamb. The nations will walk by its light, and the kings of the earth will bring their glory into it. Its gates will never be shut.... Then the angel showed me the river of the water of life, bright as crystal, flowing from the throne of God and of the Lamb through the middle of the street of the city. On either side of the river is the tree of life with its twelve kinds of fruit, producing its fruit each month; and the leaves of the tree are for the healing of the nations. Nothing accursed will be found there anymore. But the throne of God and of the Lamb will be in it, and his servants will worship him; they will see his face, and his name will be on their foreheads.[12]

The world is no longer comprised of kingdoms and countries divided from one another, but a unified city, teeming with life. It's a place of nourishment and healing for all people. Nothing is separated from God, and God is in the thick of everything. This is the future that invades the present in Jesus: face-to-face intimacy with God.

We will see God's face. This is about more than knowing what God looks like. It calls to mind Abraham who was "the friend of God" or Moses, "whom the LORD knew face to face."[13] "Knowing," biblically speaking, is always about more than information or general awareness. When Moses knew God face to face, it wasn't simply that he could give theologically sound sermons, or that he knew all of God's rules, or that he could adequately explain God to Israel. That may all be true, but more importantly, Moses knew God intimately because he spent time in God's company, learning the cadences of God's voice, growing in trust and love of God, deepening in devotion and friendship with God. What St. John describes, and what God wants, is a world in which we all "know as we are fully known."[14]

This knowing is possible because God desires it to be. From the get-go, God has refused to stay at a safe and heavenly distance from us. God has always rejected the very reasonable expectation that a deity would be aloof and indifferent to whatever is happening down in the dust of everyday life. But as we've seen in the primordial story, sin gets in the way of that God-desired intimacy. The humans choose something other than the Creator-creature relationship that is meant to be the source and sustenance of flourishing. They sabotage the relationship upon which their very lives depend. We consistently do the same.

12. Rev 21.
13. Exod 33:11.
14. 1 Cor 13:12.

And one of the reasons we know that God is not like us, is that God is relentlessly committed to having things another way than we have made them. I would have washed my hands of the whole ordeal and spent eternity in triune bliss. Not this God. This God sets to work restoring what's been lost. First, as God outlines the consequences of the situation, we hear that a descendent of Eve will destroy the serpent, the deceiver, even if the serpent gets one last bite in. There's One coming who will overcome the deception and destruction that's been unleashed, even if it kills him. And the second glimpse of hope comes as we see God, in a charming bit of poetic license, making leather garments for the yet-beloved creatures. God exchanges their silly leaf garments, and begins to cover their shame, gives them a way to walk a little more freely in the world. God clothes them.

In that act of generosity, we see that God is not satisfied to be done with humanity. While the humans are driven from the garden, and just a few verses later we see the first murder, not long after that we get the story of Noah, in which God undertakes a massive reset through the flood, there is still a glimpse of hope. It's not altogether clear how that hope will play out or how God intends to restore things to the good and very good way that they are made to be. The reset of the flood, and more importantly the covenant that God makes with Noah and his family, makes it clear that God is neither indifferent to evil, nor done with this world.

But things are still pretty vague. They become clearer when we meet Abram and Sarai, who will be Abraham and Sarah. Their story is, like any life, one of both faith and faithlessness. The Bible's witness to that fact is a means of grace, reminding us that while they are firmly among the great heroes of our faith, God's reconciling work is not dependent upon their, or our, perfection. This is God's action. That's made plain by the fact that Abraham and Sarah are utterly unlikely people to take part in God's divine scheme, which will be a consistent and beautiful pattern that continues in every generation, even today. The Bible and the church are full of unlikely saints.

Genesis 12, where the old couple's act begins, starts almost by surprise. We've heard Abram's name, and we know that Sarai is his wife before now, but there has been no indication that they would be the matriarch and patriarch of God's world-redeeming mission. There's no sense that they are remarkable people. All we know is their family tree, and the fact that they haven't been able to have any kids themselves. Then, seemingly out of the blue, we hear:

> Now the LORD said to Abram, "Go from your country and your kindred and your father's house to the land that I will show you. I will make of you a great nation, and I will bless you, and make your name great, so that you will be a blessing. I will bless those who bless you, and the one who curses you I will curse; and in you all the families of the earth shall be blessed.[15]

Perhaps even more surprising than God showing up so suddenly is that Abram listens. He does it. He packs up everything he's got, and with Sarai and his nephew Lot, heads out to . . . somewhere. It's easy for those of us who know the rest of the story well to overlook the fact that God doesn't tell Abram where he's supposed to go, only that God will show him. Making matters rather stranger is the fact that Abram is seventy-five years old, and Sarai is sixty-five, which is a little mature to start a family, let alone a great nation.

But God has promised, so they go. Only, the promise doesn't come to fruition in quite the way they had expected. They remain childless for several years yet. Tired of waiting around for God, they try to take matters into their own hands. When Abram is eighty-six years old, he has a child with Sarai's servant, Hagar. There are some remarkable things that happen in Hagar's story—not the least of which is that she is the first person in Scripture to speak God's name. But, to make perfectly clear that this is God's plan, Abram and Sarai's plotting won't do. They are not in charge of creating this great nation, the world-blessing people who will reveal God's goodness and grace. This is God's work.

Still, Abram is frustrated. It's hard to blame him. It's been many years since he gave up everything to follow God's call, and it's starting to seem like maybe he misheard. God has continued to promise that something great is coming. That God is determined to bless the world through Abram. But the old man is not so sure. And he lets God know it, with a directness that might make well-behaved church folk squirm. Rather than flick him off the face of the earth, God takes him outside one evening and tells him to count the stars, promising that his descendants will be just as numerous.

Then a weird thing happens, even by biblical standards. God tells Abram to bring some animals: a heifer, a goat, a ram, and some birds. God tells him to cut the animals in half and make a path between the parts. This is what's known as "cutting a covenant." It's what would happen when two parties entered into agreement with one another, each committing to

---

15. Gen 12:1–3.

uphold their side of the deal. The idea was that both parties, or at least the one of lower standing, would walk through this messy path as if to say: "Let this be what happens to me, if my side of the covenant breaks down. Let me be torn apart." It's intense. It's staking one's life for the sake of what's being promised.

We might reasonably think that this would be a test of Abram's faithfulness. Does he really trust God enough? Will he keep moving forward, even though the way ahead is unclear? So, we would expect to see Abram walking through the animal pieces, doubling down on his commitment to do what God wants of him. But that's not what we see at all. Instead, Abram is made to fall asleep. Only God goes through the path. It's a staggering moment.

Once again, the promise is God's. The action is God's. The faithfulness in question is God's. The determination to have a people who will show the world what it means to live in love and justice and righteousness is God's. The commitment to restoring the world, to healing the divisions that begin with our division from God, is God's. Through Abraham, through a people participating in *God's* mission, the world will be blessed. The world will be as it's meant to be. God will stake his life on the promise.

Ultimately, Abraham and Sarah do have a son so miraculous that they can only call him Laughter: Isaac. The ways and means of God are often so surprising that all we can do is marvel at the wonder of it all. When God's promises take shape in our lives, our mouths are often "filled with laughter."[16] With Isaac, the world-blessing people is begun. Isaac and his wife Rebekah have a son, Jacob. Jacob becomes the eponymous father of the tribes of Israel, who will be God's people, chosen to live in and reveal God's love to the world—like Adam and Eve were made to.

Of course, much of the story of the Bible is concerned with the fact that the descendants of Abraham and Sarah are inconsistent in their willingness to participate in God's world-blessing mission. There are some extraordinary moments of faithfulness. But there are lots of testimonies to the fact that even God's chosen people regularly choose something other than God's will and way in the world.

One of the strange things about the Bible is how open and honest it is about the fact that those whom God calls are a mixed bag of commitment and infidelity. This is a peculiar means of grace. One might expect the Scriptures to show us only the best and the brightest, the heroically

---

16. Ps 126:2.

faithful, those who unwaveringly cling to God and God's ways. Instead, it reminds us that we're in good company in both our faith and our fickleness. It's unabashed in its proclamation that we all "sin and fall short of the glory of God."[17] And it points us again and again to God's faithfulness, no matter what. God has sold out for this promise. If intimacy bookends the story of God with God's people, God's faithfulness holds it together. It's not always in the ways that we would expect, or even the ways that we'd want. But time and again the Bible brings us face to face with God's relentless determination to have the world God wants, to be—as only God can be—God *for* the world.

Even in the midst of Israel's most blatant seasons of faithlessness, the prophets continued to insist that this is the people to and through whom God would be faithful. The promise to bless the world, to restore lost intimacy, to reestablish the life-giving Creator-creature relationship with all things—for the flourishing of all things—was made to Abraham and his descendants. And this God is the God who makes promises and keeps them. Christians believe that we see God's promises culminate in a particular form, in a particular place, at a particular time, in the person and work of Jesus of Nazareth.

In Jesus, we see how far God will go to love the world. We see just how much God will give to reestablish the relationship of intimacy that is marred by sin. We see how relentlessly God will pursue what is lost, to restore us to God's good and very good will for all things. We see Jesus working for the healing and wholeness of those around him. We see him facing down systems and structures that have us chasing after idols, rather than seeking God's face. We see his call of people who don't deserve it, to draw near, to abide in his love, to give themselves in joy and gladness to one another, and to the One who has given everything for them.

We see all this come to a head on the cross, as Jesus is crucified for the sake of God's kingdom. Here, I'm assuming a robust trinitarian theology. We can trust that when the writers of the Bible promise that Jesus is the One who was with God and was God from the beginning, the word who is made flesh, that is true.[18] When the writer of Colossians sings that "in him all the fullness of God was pleased to dwell," we can trust that, even though the logistics of it bend the mind, there is something ultimately faithful about

---

17. Rom 3:23.
18. John 1:1–14.

the testimony.[19] We can count on the promise that Jesus Christ was equal with God but refused to cling to that, and instead emptied himself into this world, and as a result is the One who is even now making all things new.[20] The Bible begins with God playing in the dirt—a dirt under the fingernails kind of God. The gospels show us God with dust on his feet.

This theological claim matters because it means that what we see in Jesus's crucifixion is not simply another prophet mowed down by the world's fear and rage. He's not just another Jewish rebel taken out by the Roman Empire; he's not an idealist, crushed by the keepers of the way things are. Nor is the cross an instance of divine child abuse, or simply the substitution of one *really* good man as a scapegoat for the rest of us. The crucifixion is not satisfaction for God's bloodlust.

No. What we see in Jesus is the lengths to which God will go to overcome the distance that would destroy us. We see God's unwillingness to stay apart from us, even if it costs everything. We see on the cross God keeping his promise to be torn apart for the sake of the world-blessing covenant, and to establish a new covenant in his own body. We see God giving everything to curse what would curse us. Where the first Adam hid naked behind a tree in shame, Jesus, the new Adam, the one wholeheartedly committed to God's will and way, hangs naked on a tree and destroys shame.[21]

The cross bears witnesses to the fact that all forgiveness is costly. The reconciliation of a broken relationship is a demanding process. When we forgive, we give up our right to retaliation. When we seek reconciliation, we relinquish our anger and pain for another option. The writer of Colossians says that not only was the fullness of God pleased to dwell among us in Jesus, but that through him "God was pleased to reconcile to himself all things, whether on earth or in heaven, by making peace through the blood of his cross."[22] God is pleased to bear the cost of reconciling all things, even us.

Of course, the cross alone does not tell us that what would curse us is cursed, that shame is destroyed, or that God will give up everything to be with and for this world. The cross does not mean anything without the resurrection. It's the resurrection of Jesus that makes the church bold to say that, in Christ, there isn't anything in heaven, earth, or hell that will separate

---

19. Col 1:19.

20. Phil 2:6–11.

21. I am indebted to Rich Villodas for this insight, Vancouver School of Theology Summer School, 2020.

22. Col 1:20.

us from the love of God—not even death.[23] What's more, the church is bold to say that Jesus is not just raised from the dead but ascended to heaven's throne. His will and way are at the heart of the universe, which means that this reconciling impulse, God's desire to be reconciled to all things, *is the defining reality in which we live.*

If Jesus is Lord of all, then our deepest confidence is that there is nothing God will not do, nothing God will not give, to love us, to draw near to us, to be with us and for us. We get to live from and for that fact. We are freed from our own dead-end attempts to be gods for ourselves, trusting that in the company of Jesus, by the presence and power of the Holy Spirit, we get to live and move and have our being in the wide space of God's grace. We get to live in and for the good and very good will of God, for us and for all things. That's what it means to grab hold of life that is truly life—life abundant.

The witness of the saints in every generation, and the testimony on every page of Scripture is that this God chooses to self-reveal, to be known. This God refuses to stay away. Both Israel and the church are committed to saying something about what that means, giving voice and lived expression to the fact that God so loves this world. This is the theme that holds the story together from beginning to end.

In a world where we are fractured and fragmented, divided in so many ways, the beauty of God's gathering up all things in love is very good news. In a time and place when many of us and our neighbors feel deeply disconnected, lonely, and inadequate, the gospel promises that in Christ we are being put back together, drawn into an infinite love, and cherished always. In Jesus, God has established the conditions for us to be most completely and freely who we are made to be: breathtaking creatures in relationship with our Creator; humans fully alive.

As we learn to live in these gospel conditions, we become more and more aware that this is not simply about self-improvement, living our best life, or being "hashtag blessed." It's about living as we're made to live, in and for the sake of the world. We grow to participate in God's reconciling mission. We, made in God's image, have been given a ministry of reconciliation. Far from being a solitary spiritual reality, our relationship with God must find expression in all the ways that we live and move and have our being.

I love Frederick Beuchner's insight:

23. Rom 8:31–39.

The final secret, I think, is this: that the words "You shall love the Lord your God" become in the end less a command than a promise. And the promise is that, yes, on the weary feet of faith and the fragile wings of hope, we will come to love him at last as from the first he has loved us—loved us even in the wilderness, especially in the wilderness, because he has been in the wilderness with us. He has been in the wilderness for us.[24]

Our Relationship with Ourselves

In the Genesis story, the emphasis is on the failure of humanity to live in right relationship with God. That's right and good. It should be our primary concern. But honestly, it's not the part that gets me. Perhaps that's because I grew up in the church, and even during my paltry attempts at rebellion in young adulthood I never really struggled to trust in God's intimacy, and the tenacity of God's forgiveness. The reality and closeness of God is the environment I came of age in. I count myself awfully lucky in that.

It's the entry of shame into the world that strikes more directly at my experience. The contrast between humanity naked and unashamed, and then suddenly cowering, desperately covering themselves for fear of being fully seen—my guess is that that's about as universal an image as there is. The covering up in each other's presence to hide their shame is qualitatively different than the act of hiding in guilt. The immediate implication of the humans trying to avoid God's gaze is that they recognize their disobedience and the inevitability of consequences. God told them not to eat of the Tree of the Knowledge of Good and Evil, and they did so anyway. They know their guilt before the LORD.

But guilt is not shame. They often accompany each other, but they are not the same thing: guilt is feeling badly about what we've done; shame is feeling badly about who we are. Guilt makes us hide behind a tree, where we are fairly easily found. Shame coerces a disguise, demands a cover-up. Guilt can be useful for helping us know when we have acted out of line with the way we're made, and it is reasonably easily dealt with. Misdeeds can be admitted to, forgiveness sought. Amends can be made and justice served. There may not always be a perfectly straightforward answer to the problem of guilt, but in general we can discern a reasonable course of action to set things right. Shame entwines itself around our cores.

24. Buechner, "Final Secret."

Psychiatrist Curt Thompson wonders what might have happened, how the story might have been different, if the humans had just acknowledged their disobedience.[25] Knowing, as Jews and Christians have come to, that God is the One who is "slow to anger and abounding in steadfast love," the One who "does not treat us as our sins deserve,"[26] what might have happened if they had simply confessed? Possibly nothing different. The story still abounds in grace—which is not the absence of consequences. But we'll never know.

Because it is clear that there is something in the humans' behavior that belies the fact that they believe something is fundamentally altered. They are different than they were. Once they were naked and unashamed. No more. Shame has its way. And unlike guilt, shame is never useful.[27] Shame doesn't reveal what's wrong, it lies about what's right. Guilt, once acknowledged, might move us toward God and neighbor in repentance. Shame is invariably isolating. Guilt reveals our weaknesses and allows us to address them. Shame does everything it can to mask our vulnerability.

But we are not made for isolation. Thompson says beautifully that "we come into the world looking for someone looking for us."[28] That's not just a lovely metaphor for our deep need for love. We know, scientifically, that babies, almost from the first breath outside the womb, respond to a face directed at them.[29] Soon they are most comforted by the face of someone who loves them. Adam's outburst of joy at the first sight of Eve is poetic, but also paradigmatic. The relief of an appropriate partner, someone who can see him with an intimate gaze, is palpable. We're meant for joy in the presence of others. That it's not good for us to be alone is one of the first things the Bible tells us about ourselves. Created in the image of the One who is eternally communal, we are made for fulsome partnership with others. We're meant to be open and vulnerable and intimate, "naked" with one another. God doesn't become a garment worker until after shame has its way with us.

But our widespread, Western cultural inclination toward self-protection and individualism is indicative that shame runs rampant and keeps us in hiding. Even in many churches the unwillingness or inability to share

---

25. Thompson, "What Is Shame?"
26. Ps 103.
27. Contra Thompson, *Soul of Shame*, 76.
28. Thompson, "What Is Shame?"
29. Horowitz, *On Looking*, 84.

our weaknesses, fears, and needs is evidence that we are not prepared to be completely in each other's presence. As a pastor, I have had a front-row seat to witness the hesitancy of folks to say what's really going on, to share struggles, or admit failures. And I've succumbed to that fear, many times.

On the other hand, one of the curious things over the past several years is the emergence of a style of social media post that evokes the vulnerability—or our more preferred, "authenticity"—without being truly vulnerable. Such posts purportedly create a better connection with one's audience. "Getting real" gives the impression that we are seeing something that is real and true. The obvious irony is that carefully curated moments of authenticity are not authentic. From the moment one chooses to send such a post into the ether it's inherently offered from a distance, with decisions being made about presentation and minimal on-the-ground relational consequences. Followers affirm from afar, liking but not truly loving; trolls may hurt our feelings but don't become enemies we need to learn to love in real time and space. It's hard to avoid the sense that authenticity is essentially marketable. The choice to present as "vulnerable" on a platform at the very core of which is artifice, is a strange but lucrative one.

The trouble is, we don't choose to be vulnerable. We *are* vulnerable.[30] It's how we're made: naked and unashamed. And we need spaces, relationships, communities in which that is truly possible—where we can bring our whole selves into the light of day, not for cheap voyeurism, but for our healing and wholeness. Like the church.

Shame hinders relationships that are truly healing and whole, largely because it hinders our capacity to tell the truth about ourselves to each other.[31] There's a reason that many people find Alcoholics Anonymous more transformative and restorative than your average church: because the only way to get through the program is to tell the truth. And truth, it turns out, will set you free.

It sets us free because there is no way to tell the truth about ourselves that will leave us in shame. It will reveal our guilt, it will unearth some junk we'd like to keep hidden or that we've managed to forget about. But ultimately, if we tell the truth enough, in brave spaces with others, it will get us back to the fact of ourselves: that we are made in, with, and for the love of God; that we are known and delighted in by the maker of heaven and earth. That's where our anthropology begins. It's what we're meant for.

30. Thompson, *Soul*, 120.
31. Thompson, *Soul*, 67.

This is why confessing our sins is one of the gifts of the church. Confession helps us recognize that every one of us is both beautiful and broken, each navigating all the same basic obstacles to being fully human. Communal confession—acknowledging our sin with and in the presence of others—also tells us an important truth: sin isn't interesting.

I've had the chance to sit in a group on a couple of occasions for the sole purpose of confessing our sins to one another. And the remarkable thing is that sin is mostly boring. The stuff we'd keep hidden isn't worthy of the effort. Of course, there's often titillation in the moment; we wouldn't do these things if they didn't seem fun. But as a rule, it's all variation on a handful of tired themes. Get three people together and there's a real good chance that they all know something about struggling with purity of heart and gaze; they all know something about anger and greed and malice. The devil is just not creative. But he is, according to the story, crafty. We are up against the "wiles of the devil."[32] Even in mainline traditions, where we don't talk much about evil and spiritual warfare and the devil, I'm pretty sure that honesty would compel most of us to admit that we know what Paul is on about when he says that whenever he wants to do good, evil seems to be lurking around the corner. The good he wants to do, he doesn't; the junk he wants to avoid, he can't.[33]

I preach regularly about extravagant forgiveness and loving our enemies, and I want to be the kind of person who does that. And I also spend embarrassing amounts of time rehearsing the devastating things I'd like to say to those who've hurt me. And it's frustratingly, painfully easy for those harsh, bitter, even hateful things to get into my head.

I really do want to believe that everyone I meet is made in the image of God. But I live in a place where it rains a lot, and lots of people have these ridiculously oversized umbrellas that take up three times the space a person on the sidewalk should. It sets me ablaze with righteous indignation. There's a little part of me that thinks it'd be a good idea to lower my shoulder and run them over. That's a fairly tame example. I could go on. And on. The good I would do, I don't; what I wouldn't do, I do. I'm easily distracted from the Way of Jesus.

The serpent is craftier than the other creatures, but his tactic is transparent: isolation. When evil enters the scene, the serpent gets Eve on her own, convinces her to question her standing with God, seduces her into

32. Eph 6:11.
33. Rom 7:15–16.

believing that her beloved creatureliness isn't enough, and compels her to strive to be something she is not and was never meant to be. The human's isolation begins the movement away from God, her true self, her partner, and the good world of God's creation. The man follows quickly behind her, and they are alone together.[34]

St. Peter's simile for evil gets at the same point when he says that the devil is like a ravaging lion, looking for prey to devour.[35] The lion's tactic is to isolate the prey from the pack, exposing its vulnerability and making it an easy target. Sin makes us feel alone, as if we are the only ones who would do this or feel that way. And loneliness is the rich soil in which shame grows. When we confess our sins to God and each other, we choose to move toward instead of away. Confession and the grace that follows give us the security of the pack. It allows us to say to one another: you're still part of us, you're still loved, you are forgiven. When we bring our guilt into God's presence together, we're trusting the One who promises that we will be cleansed of all unrighteousness.[36] When we confess our sin in spaces, relationships, and communities where we can bring our whole selves, then we move toward the One who will cross heaven and earth to move toward us.

Ideally, our liturgies and practices help us move more and more deeply into the reality that ultimately God speaks more truthfully than the serpent's story. God tells a better story than our limited versions of reality. We learn again to hear the cadence and rhythm, to know the arc of God's story. Within that story, we learn to tell the truth about ourselves and this God-beloved world, and the truth will be beautiful. When we are forgiven, we get to feel God's sigh of delight over us: the promise that by grace we and this world are made good and very good.[37] That's what's truest about us.

In the end, receiving that grace—the gift of our true selves—is how we are most able to do what Jesus tells us to do: to love God with everything we

---

34. It seems to me that St. Paul is missing the mark when he condemns Eve for being deceived—and that's why somehow women are misrepresented as the weaker sex (1 Tim 2:14). Eve caved under the weight of the devil's craftiness; Adam just needed to have the fruit handed to him. We men will often trade our birthright for a snack.

35. 1 Pet 5:8.

36. 1 John 1:9.

37. All confession needs to be followed by an assurance that we are indeed forgiven, that God's deep desire is not to punish, but to cleanse. Smith, *You Are What You Love*, 109–10.

are and have, and love our neighbors as ourselves.[38] We can love God and others only to the degree that we are known by God and others. Love is the condition in which we are naked and unashamed: vulnerable, connected, and fully alive.[39]

Our Relationship with Others

There's a woman I come across now and then on social media, who posts videos about how she and her husband maintain their happy and healthy Christian marriage. One talking point that she regularly revisits is the fact that she and her spouse do not have any personal private interactions with members of the opposite sex. The notion being: the absence of temptation will protect the sanctity of their marriage.

I can imagine some wisdom in that decision, but mostly I think it's naïve, because the absence of temptation doesn't equate to the absence of sin. The issue is clearly the sins of lust, adultery, and covenant unfaithfulness—about which Jesus is clear: you don't have to do much to get caught up in those things.[40] What's more, if sin is the unravelling of relationships, then the righteous choice—bearing witness to the forgiveness of sins—cannot be the refusal of relationships. It needs to be the transformation of them.

Sticking with the paradigm of Genesis 3, while I believe that the breakdown of Adam and Eve's relationship is about more than dysfunction between men and women, it's worth starting there. Clearly in the wake of the #MeToo and #ChurchToo movements, and the ongoing and regular revelation of gender-based discrimination, abuse, and violence in nearly every institution and structure we've got, we are not at liberty anymore to pretend as though things are alright between the sexes—even if we might have expected to be more enlightened and well-behaved by now. We don't seem to outgrow sin.

Adam's response, when God questions him, plants the weed of misogyny that never gets fully uprooted in Scripture, and consequently continues to spread today.[41] It was all the fault of "this woman that you gave me." It's

---

38. Mark 12:31.

39. Curt Thompson writes: "We are maximally creative when we are simultaneously maximally vulnerable and intimately connected, and evil knows this." (Thompson, *Soul*, 99.) It seems to me that creativity and love go theologically hand-in-hand.

40. Matt 5:28.

41. I do believe that there are resources in Scripture to help us confess, repent of,

hard not to hear the depersonalizing, even dehumanizing, tone in his voice. He won't say her name. He speaks as if she's not standing right there. He's humiliated but there will be no humility. Only blame. No longer breathless with love poetry, this line is venomously spit.

At the root of every act of misogyny or misanthropy is this impulse to depersonalization and, ultimately, dehumanization. When Jesus tells his disciples that when a man looks at a woman with lust (one misogynistic outworking) that man commits adultery in his heart, he's aiming at that root. It's worth distinguishing lust from attraction. Lust is not a problem of attraction. Surely Jesus cannot be expecting that we avoid any feelings of attraction, acknowledgment of beauty, or even desire, since the continuation of our species seems to depend on these things.

Instead, lust is the choice to reduce another to an object meant for one's own pleasure and possession. The whole person is traded for a partial version of themselves that conforms to the particular and selfish desires of the onlooker. Lust has no mutuality. It's devoid of intimacy. It is pure objectification and total reduction.[42] It is impossible to treat someone as a divine image-bearer if you reduce them to their genitals—or whatever part has caught your eye.

My generation and those that followed have grown up with easy access to portrayals of every sexual act and fantasy. Sex is ubiquitous. The likelihood that your average ten-year-old has been subjected to pornographic imagery of some kind is shudderingly high. Which means, if nothing else, that many people are shaped from an early age—catechized, to use some appropriate churchy language—to understand sexual relationships according to the skewed expectations of pornographic faux-sex/sexuality. Children are being trained to believe that scripted, often air-brushed and multi-take, ever-available sexual encounters are legitimate forms of intimacy.

Obviously, I can only speak about the disordering experience of growing up in a pornographized culture from my limited male, straight, cisgender perspective.[43] But even so, I know that the damage is wide-

---

and heal from the damage of misogyny—because I believe that God's deep desire is the flourishing and freedom of all people. Nevertheless, there are plenty of passages, easily isolated and pressed into service for systems that elevate men and subjugate women.

42. This is the problem with consuming pornography. It's not that sex is bad or shameful. Sex is beautiful and God-given. But the assumed voyeurism of porn reduces the participants to their physical attributes, disregarding their personhood, and as a result often results in violence and brutality toward women. Wallace, "Big Red Son," 3–50.

43. Improbable relational and physical expectations are not limited to the private

spread, verging on universal. Recently, multi-award-winning singer and songwriter Billie Eilish publicly acknowledged the significant damage that early exposure to and frequent consumption of pornography inflicted on her expectations about relationships.[44] When even the rock stars start to cry out, perhaps we'll listen.

Personally, I'm grateful for the women who have forged friendships with me and enriched my life immeasurably by doing so. Many, if not most, of those women are colleagues and followers of Jesus. That's a gift, because church needs to be a place where we can cultivate spiritual energy that is not confused with sexual energy. I'm grateful to have partnered with a wife with whom I have discovered what whole and wholesome relationship is, and who values the benefits of my friendships with other women. I'm grateful that ours is the God who tenaciously undermines our predisposition to reduce others to some personally benefiting function.

Which leads to the fact that while the church needs to have something to say about pornography and its attendant sins, if for no other reason than the fact that it is nearly unavoidable—hopefully something more nuanced than so-called "purity culture" and more urgent than the shoulder-shrugging silence of more liberal limbs of the body—it is nevertheless awfully low-hanging fruit. Lust is only one kind of reductionism of our image-of-God neighbors, and pornography only one manifestation of it. Our reduction of others plays out in every other unraveled relationship.

Which means that the problem is not just between genders. It's interpersonal. We do it all the time. We fail to marvel at our neighbors, to delight in the sheer fact of them. Instead of mutuality, we default to selfishness. But, Jesus says, in the same sermon in which he speaks so harshly about lust, that calling our neighbor a fool—reducing them to their actions, or our interpretation of their actions—is every bit as damnable as inappropriately fantasizing about them.[45] His instructions about anger eliminate our option to pursue self-righteousness against those with whom we have one sort of beef or another.[46] What he says about generosity denies us the opportunity to reduce others to our metrics of worthiness.[47] By the end of the Sermon

---

pornographic indulgences—they're everywhere, from advertisements and video games to sports magazines and social media, and just about everywhere else we look.

44. "Billie Eilish."
45. Matt 5:22.
46. Matt 5:22.
47. Matt 5:42.

on the Mount there's not much wiggle room to engage with our neighbors with anything less than divine seriousness. Over and over again we're compelled to behold others in love, to move toward our troublesome siblings when we'd rather do away with them, and to refuse to reduce them to the size of our expectations and our fickle and fraught desires.

So, how do we overcome our natural—or at least sinful—tendency to treat others according to the myopic limitations of their utility or our fancy, to deal with our neighbors, partners, family, and friends, as anything less than divine gift? Biblically, the practical answer is self-giving love worked out in acts of service. We are made in, through, and for the One who's plan for salvation is mostly a willingness to give up power, embrace vulnerability even if it kills him, and commit to that posture right to the end and then through it. The strange good news of Jesus Christ is that we are set free in this world—free for God, for our truest selves—not so that we can do whatever we want, but so that we can do what we're made to do: outdo one another in love.[48]

One thinker on these things says that the answer to the dehumanization of porn is soup kitchens: Sharing a table with strangers, who are of no obvious benefit to you except that they are made in God's image—and will teach you something about that image in all their marvelous and infuriating humanity.[49] It's hard to imagine anything more contrary to the private, self-indulgent, diminishment of pornography than participating in a meal with folks who can't do anything for you, except eat with you. Only, I think this sort of thing is more than an antidote to the disease of porn; this is really just the way Jesus tells us to be. He regularly tells his disciples to both submit themselves to the generosity of others, and to give of their time, energy, and resources for those who can't return the favor; to go beyond rational relational limitations, so that we might see what happens on the other side of our expectations. Our being responsible to and for others is a key element in his salvation strategy: it's how we get close to the kingdom of God.

This is at least part of what St. Paul is on about when he tells us not to be conformed to the patterns of this world—often marked by selfish ambition and greed, violence and dismissiveness—but let our minds be transformed for the sake of what God is up to, which is always love, justice, and

---

48. Gal 5:13; Rom 12:10.
49. I heard this from Jason Byassee, who credits Amy Frykholm.

righteousness.[50] It's no wonder that Paul's encouragement to "outdo one another in showing honor" follows close behind the call for a new imagination for the way things really are. What if the church was a place where we learned to one-up each other in recognizing the wonder and glory, the fearful miracle of every person we meet? This really is an improbably beautiful tactic for living more humanly with one another, instead of the fragmented ways of life that we are regularly encouraged toward. Contrary to so much social media and self-help noise about striving after our (self-defined) best selves, our Lord tells us to get after the glory of others.

What would it look like if we took these holy strategies out of the church and into our everyday lives? If classrooms were spaces for mutuality and encouragement? If we expected checkout lines to be sites of divine encounter? If a corporate office was a place in which everyone was encouraged to seek, and celebrated for pursuing the well-being and flourishing of their colleagues, and all those with whom their business deals? What would our households, or classrooms, or gyms look like if we strove to outdo one another in honor?

One of the many things I've learned from my father-in-law is that one way to learn to love people is to serve them. More than anyone I've ever known, he will go out of his way for the sake of another. And as far as I can tell, it's never an inconvenience to him, even when it is obviously inconvenient. It's just a matter of course. It's what you do. The remarkable thing is that when we serve others out of a desire to care for them (as opposed to doing it for some ulterior motive, like approval or manipulation) we end up actually caring for them. When we serve our spouses, or children, or friends, or coworkers, out of a desire for their best, resentment flees. It's just a delight to delight them.

It becomes impossible to reduce someone to the level of our expectations, or desires, or their utility when we cultivate the instinct to honor, and then honor some more. Honoring others makes possible all the wild things that Jesus tells us we have to do: forgive relentlessly, give extravagantly, love reflexively, hope lavishly. It enables us to behold another, to take seriously the fact that the God who made the heavens and the earth is pleased to be imaged in this improbable being, pleased to be magnified in their souls, pleased to know their name and every hair on their heads. Honoring others is the way for us to see them as the God-beloved creature that they are. And,

---

50. Rom 10:2.

as Brian Doyle puts it, "Sometimes we are starving to see every bit of what is right in front of us."[51]

Our Relationship with Nonhuman Creation

When I arrived at my church there was someone who was part of the congregation, who was particularly passionate about environmental justice. The first time we met was to discuss her involvement with a Christian environmental organization, and her desire to see our church linked up with it. Part of me was taken with her enthusiasm. When someone is deeply passionate about a thing, it's hard not to be drawn in. And I, like any good left-leaning Christian, think that care of creation is important. I have all the time in the world for organizations like *A Rocha*, that wed commitments to Jesus and ecology.[52] I know Jesus talked about plants a lot. On the other hand, part of me was also wary, as she outlined her ideas for "greening" our church. I began to have visions of exchanging the Revised Common Lectionary for readings from the Global Environmental Accord series.[53]

I know plenty of mainline churches whose identity is deeply rooted in a particular cause or social justice initiative. And sometimes it's not altogether clear whether their primary commitment is to issue X or to Jesus Christ. But I want to be a church focused on discipleship to Jesus. I want to make sure we are worshiping the God who made creation—not giving God props when it helps an environmental cause. I want people to be caught up in the movement of the Spirit and from there be compelled to care for whatever little plot of creation we find ourselves in.

As time went on she'd raise her voice at meetings, pepper prayers with pleas for creation and that we would wake from our collective indifference. Eventually, she and her husband left in search of another church that is more aligned with their commitments and passions. And in the end, I was left wondering if she was on to something that I simply missed.

I'm still skeptical of churches that gather mostly around a cause. There are organizations that will address those concerns more effectively and with better branding, and folks should definitely give their time and energy there. As the church, all we have to offer, that no one else does better, is Jesus.

51. Doyle, *One Long River*, 7.
52. Kostamo, *Planted*.
53. Choucri, ed., "Environmental Accord."

But the reality is that the things that we do with our bodies, our time, our money—the ways that we live and move and have our being in the world—are the only evidence of what we truly believe. And if it's true that all creation is groaning, waiting for the children of God to get our collective act together, then rolling our eyes at someone's passion about an issue as unquestionably urgent as climate change is not evidence that we're more committed to lofty things.[54] It's more likely a failure of nerve. We know, as God's people always have, that if we listen to the prophets we'll have to change.

More than self-preservation is at stake. We should take seriously the wryest predictions from those in the scientific community who are certain that the world will outlast our current rate of damage, even if we won't. But we're called to something deeper than ensuring we make it. We're called to partake in divine delight, to play our role in the very good order that things are made for.[55]

Rabbi Abraham Heschel says, "Wonder or radical amazement is the chief characteristic of the religious man's attitude toward history and nature."[56] Wonder and radical amazement. Restoring our relationship with creation is less a practical consideration than an invitation into a profound and loving astonishment at all God has done. It's to take seriously the miracle of things, the fact of anything when there could be nothing. It's to pay attention to the biblical truth that humanity is not the only revelation of God's being and nature. It's worth noting that we don't even get our own day of creation. On the sixth day, we get created with all the rest of the animals—different, sure, but undeniably bound up in the wonder and well-being of all God's creatures. It's a literary testimony to the fact that we are not to imagine ourselves outside or above the rest of creation.

Psalm 19 invites us to pay attention to a creation that declares God's glory, in deep conversation with the Word that was from the beginning. The rather bawdy image of the sun springing forth like a bridegroom after his wedding night tells us something about the enthusiasm with which we ought to greet the day but also the way that the day greets us. There is a whole world eager to tell us about the love it has known. The sun, apparently, kisses and tells. It tells of an anticipated generativity and creativity, an expectation that the world will teem with life. Pope John Paul II says, "A

---

54. Rom 8:19–23.
55. Harper, *Very Good Gospel*; Genesis 1.
56. Heschel, "Radical Amazement."

new dimension of God's glory begins with the creation of the visible and invisible world."[57] Like every human we encounter, the whole created world, in all its splendor, is meant to reveal something precious to God's heart.

Of course, the reality of sin is not just a problem for us humans, but it pervades all of creation. There is brokenness and dysfunction all over the place. It's telling that when Isaiah envisions a peaceable kingdom, it's not just humans who will learn war no more, but animals that are "natural" enemies find themselves somehow reconciled. The lion and the lamb will lie down together; adders and wolves will live in unexpected harmony, they will be perfect playmates for children.

In St. John's great final vision of the world as God wants it, we're told that there is no more sea. This isn't an anti-marine sentiment. God loves and delights in the waters of the earth. But the sea was an image of chaos, danger, unpredictability, and disorder to the folks John was pastoring. In the world renewed, those real and present fears are evaporated. We'll be eternally in the company of the One who commands the waves to be at peace. It's an image of the whole world healed and in harmony with heaven's song.

The Genesis vision of humanity's relationship with creation was for us to participate in maintaining that song from the start. We were meant to do the work of keeping things in the right key, at the right tempo, adding our own musical texture but never abandoning the original tune. We were meant to participate in creating and sustaining the conditions for flourishing, for giving voice and expression to the glory of the One from whose heart the whole cosmos overflowed.

A corrective to our distorted relationship with nonhuman creation is to meditate on ancient prayers like Psalm 8. Joining our hearts and souls to the communion of saints that has sung and prayed this psalm for millennia, draws us into the company of those who have rightly understood our place within God's good creation. The invitation to look up beyond ourselves and embrace our smallness, to recognize God's ultimate glory, is a first step in undermining the hubris that would have us treating creation as ours to exploit. Though verses 5–8 suggest an elevated status for humans within the order of things, it is more properly pointing to a vocational reality: it reminds the worshiping community that we are made in God's image, created to reflect God's goodness and care for all things, stewarding all that God has given.

---

57. John Paul II, "Creation Reveals."

In many ways, the problems faced by those of us living in the wake of the industrial revolution are radically different from and surely beyond imagining for those who first bore witness to God's glory in creation, whose testimony fills the pages of Scripture. But there is evidence that the machinations of every empire have left the scars of outsized ambition on the earth.[58] Our relentless desire to imagine ourselves above the rest of creation, rather than integrally within and mutually dependent upon it, has always distorted and disrupted the abundant life conditions that God intended.

That said, the way our communities respond here and now to the environmental degradation that threatens countless species including our own, ought to embody an appropriate urgency. What's more, people being shaped in the Way of Jesus ought to be deeply suspicious of the consistent political rhetoric about balancing environmental protections with the expectation that the economy—which is literally a figment of our imaginations, not an unstoppable force—will and must expand eternally. Consistently, Jesus undermined the systems and structures, including the economy, that contributed to the disruption of God's desired shalom—that deep flourishing that is at the heart of all divine commitment.

To respond to current environmental challenges, we almost certainly need to embrace the kind of downward mobility that marked the culture of the early church.[59] We might need to take a page out of the "Redemptive Entrepreneurship" playbook, willingly refusing the relentless pursuit of profit and self-interest for the sake of delighting in the kind of world that is freed to proclaim the glory of God with everything it's got.[60]

This needs to be a communal effort. We cannot address massive challenges on our own. Surely, every little bit counts. But our capacity to participate in God's work of restoration and renewal is, like everything else in God's economy, a relational work. Left to our own devices, most of us will certainly end up discouraged and fearful that our meager efforts won't

---

58. Keesmaat and Walsh, *Romans Disarmed*, 210.

59. I recently heard Canadian environmental activist, David Suzuki, express a measure of hope that we truly do not have sufficient knowledge to know how bad the damage we have done is. So, I want to think about what faces us as challenges, rather than crises. I do not think this is wishful thinking. Creation has generally shown itself to be remarkably resilient. And ours is the God of resurrection. Lament and repentance should mark our current stance toward environmental issues. But so should hope and a vigorous embrace of the God-given gifts and capacities we have for creating and maintaining the conditions for a Genesis-style, "very good" flourishing.

60. "What Is Redemptive Entrepreneurship?"

amount to much. We're much more likely to shrug our shoulders in despair on our own.

I wonder in what creative ways we could encourage one another to a more robust care for and delight in creation. It is easy to find ourselves overwhelmed by the magnitude of the challenges surrounding human-induced climate change. Though urgent and significant changes need to be made, most of us do not have sufficient influence on our own to affect them. Given that, I am drawn to Mark Scandrette's idea of gospel "experiments."[61] These communally discerned experiments are a way of making small, biblically informed changes that can yield results much greater than our limited efforts. As well, they are a means by which we might inspire others to similar intentional choices. For instance, could we establish a practice, even for a season, of working together to offset our carbon footprints? If someone in my community is required to travel by air for work, or has the opportunity to travel for holidays, might I and others commit to a "carbon fast" to account for the added pollution? Might we commit to funding an environmental assessment of our buildings? Or covenant with one another toward mutually established and enlivening goals? Or encourage one another toward a more plant-based diet? What is God inviting your community to try out?

The testimony of Scripture and the very fact that we trust that God is the Creator of all that is means that we must not relegate forgiveness of sins to a merely spiritual or even interpersonal category. If the evidence of God's salvation drawing near is the whole creation breaking into song, we, who believe that salvation has come in Christ, had best be living toward the conditions for that singing.[62]

---

61. Scandrette, *Practicing the Way of Jesus*.
62. See, for instance, Psalm 96.

Chapter 5

Ascension

> Forerunner of mankind
> For us he reigns on high,
> Till all his members join'd
> Repeat the joyful cry
> Wide open throw the heavenly scene,
> Receive the sons of glory in![1]

> When he had made purification for sins, he sat down at the right hand of the Majesty on high, having become as much superior to angels as the name he has inherited is more excellent than theirs.
>
> HEBREWS 1:3B–4

JESUS'S CALL AND COMMISSION to proclaim repentance and the forgiveness of sins comes to a head in his ascension into heaven. I've come to love the doctrine of the ascension. I'm convinced that it is the most important doctrine that the mainline church actively ignores. But we ignore it to our peril. We need these foundational doctrines of the church—the trellis on which Christian faith and practice grow and bloom—because they give us

---

1. Wesley, "Hymns for Ascension-Day."

an essential reason and bolstered confidence to care about the things we care about. Our wildest claims are at the heart of our good news.

I understand why we ignore the ascension. We do so, I think, because it's sort of embarrassing. In our scientific culture, we're acutely aware that people do not, as a rule, float off into heaven. Even cosmologically it's a little awkward. We know, with a fair degree of certainty, that heaven is not located directly above the Mount of Olives. And even though you can go to the mount today and see what eager tourists are told are the footprints left in the rock from when Jesus blasted off to the right hand of the Father, I would have to count myself among those who are cynical about religious tourism and its more fanciful claims.

And yet. As we work to live out what it means to be people who bear the name of Jesus in the world—witnesses of repentance and the forgiveness of sins, in his name—we can't simply ignore the biblical testimony. While it is easier to treat that testimony as the work of either clever storytellers, or charmingly naïve ancients who simply didn't understand the world as well as we enlightened moderns do, the way that the biblical evangelists tell this part of the Jesus story undermines easy dismissal. Unexpectedly, they invite our disbelief and skepticism, and then draw us into the deeper and far more interesting reality that we are caught up with the God who does more than we expect: a God who gladly shows us more than we'd imagine; a God who moves between heaven and earth with startling ease.

Among the gospel writers, only Luke deals explicitly with the ascension—assuming that we accept, along with most biblical scholars, that the "shorter" and "longer" endings of Mark are later additions. But even if Mark's original manuscript ended at 16:8 with the women leaving terrified and telling no one, we are left with the awkward reality that in fact the women must have told somebody and that rather more happened than we've been told. At the very least, it's hard to explain the emergence of the church if they just walked away and kept their terrified silence.

Matthew, for his part, ends with Jesus's staggering commitment to be with us until the end of the age. Though I think that this is a beautiful, reality-shaping truth, there are days when I wonder if this is more threat than promise. The implications of Jesus's presence with us demands a kind of allegiance and obedience that is not always evident in the life of the church. Though he does not bother to elaborate on the logistics of that presence, Jesus is clearly both gone and not gone. Again, we're left with more questions than answers.

ASCENSION

In typically nonconformist fashion, John ends his gospel with an entirely different series of events. And yet, we hear the intriguing question to Peter on Jesus's lips: "If it is my will that [the beloved disciple] remain *until I come*, what is that to you?"[2] While it's not clear where Jesus is planning to go, in context we can be pretty sure it's not just a road trip. This is a rather more serious leaving from which he will return. We have questions.

At first blush, Luke's telling of the ascension seems to provide some answers. It's worth paying attention to the fact that it is so important to Luke that he tells of it twice. Except that, between his Gospel and volume 2, the book of Acts, the details change in blatantly obvious ways. The evangelist is a master storyteller, so it seems unlikely that he simply forgot what he wrote the first time around. What seems more likely to me is that Luke recognized that, even in a prescientific world, folks were aware that people did not generally launch off beyond the clouds. Luke makes plain that, although this is essential, the details are hard to pin down. We are meant to be sympathetic to the disciples who are left staring, dumbfounded, into the heavens.[3] We are meant to find ourselves alongside them.

Rather than providing answers, I have to wonder if Luke's playing with the details isn't an invitation to lean into the mystery of it all. Luke invites our skepticism by showing us something in such a way that we're not sure we can trust our senses. He is clearly not bothered by the friction in his own witness, which should make us comfortable to acknowledge that we don't really get it either. All we can say for sure is that something happened that is utterly integral to everything that happened afterwards.

Undoubtedly, the ascension stretches our modern sensibilities, but I'm inclined to agree with Leonard Sweet when he says that, as often as not, "modern Christianity is more modern than Christian."[4] This is especially true in the mainline church, where we tend to be antsy or dismissive about anything that would make our secular neighbors side-eye or dismiss us. We flatten and tame any possibility that there is more going on in the cosmos than we can, or ever will, get a handle on. I have a friend who recently told me about sitting through a sermon in which a tangential mention of the resurrection was followed with, "just so you know, that's impossible." As far as she could tell, the point was not that the impossibility of it is what makes it so incredible, but that nothing that contradicts our modern scientific

---

2. John 21:23, italics added.
3. Acts 1:11.
4. Carpenter, "Gospel," para. 15.

understandings is a legitimate claim. It's at best a projection of our deepest desires. But if we want to bear witness to something that is more than "pretty good news" we need to embrace a language and liturgy that helps us talk about what our weird claims mean, and that nurture an imagination for what breathtakingly good news it is if this stuff is somehow true.[5]

Of course, we want people to know that they are welcome in our communities and congregations irrespective of their theological commitments. I know I believe these things differently than some of the people who worship in my church every week. But I also believe it would be something awfully captivating if we thought we could do more than say, "Come as you are; stay as you were." Why not invite people into something more than they are expecting?

Let's recall that St. Paul says that his work is "the defense and confirmation of the gospel." It's work that the Philippian Christians—and we, by Holy Spirit extension—are caught up in as well. While in some traditions they're really good at *defending* the gospel, but not so hot on confirming it, in the mainline we're sometimes better at *confirming* the gospel—living it out—but stumble over its defense—we have a clear sense of what we're supposed to do, but not always why we're supposed to do it.

Honestly, I'd much rather be in the latter category. I'm not always the biggest fan of apologetics, the practice of arguing for our theological claims with cool reason. I don't think that God needs us to prove anything on his behalf. Jesus didn't spend his time convincing people with theological treatises. I love that Luke doesn't try to explain the resurrection or the ascension. Instead, he writes the book of Acts.

He tells us the story of a gaggle of nobodies caught up in the wild love of God for this world—a love fiercer than death. He tells the story of a little community on the edge of the Roman Empire that would rather die for their conviction that it's the Lamb of God, not Caesar, who is truly Lord of lords than live otherwise. He tells us the story of sinners and tax collectors, fishermen and prostitutes, theology professors and busboys, businesswomen and pimply faced teenagers, who start to take seriously the news that we live in a world in which Jesus Christ is raised from the dead and seated on

---

5. "Imagination" is not make-believe, but that gracious faculty that allows us to "apprehend more than cool reason can ever comprehend," as Shakespeare puts it. I'm indebted to Malcolm Guite for this insight. I heard him offer it during the Laing Lecture series, at Regent College, Vancouver, British Columbia, 2019. See also, Guite, *Faith, Hope and Poetry*, 55–66.

ASCENSION

heaven's throne: a world in which God will get God's way and nothing, not even death, will stop it.

Luke tells us that this improbable band of no-names and ne'er-do-wells turned the world upside down.[6] Which is really to say, they turned it right side up. They caused all sorts of holy mischief.[7] They got into all manner of gracious trouble, letting the Way of Jesus have its way in every corner of their lives.

So, I don't think that our faith is an intellectual exercise in convincing our friends and neighbors with clever arguments that what we believe is right. And even as someone who's paid to study and preach, I can get tongue-tied when someone in the pub asks some version of "well what about *this*?!" I would rather live a life of quiet witness than get into theological debates. Sure, I'm always ready to give a defense of what gives me hope, should anyone think to ask.[8] But I'm all right if they don't bother.

Still, whatever I'd prefer, I'm more and more convinced that we need to develop a facility with some language about these things. Churches need to be training grounds for talking about what it means to say that the biblical witness is, in some way—more than analogically—true. We need a fresh boldness and urgency that goes beyond quiet witness. And that may simply mean developing a comfort with saying, "I don't know." We need to allow that uncertainty is a perfectly legitimate theological answer, without allowing that the truth of the whole thing is at stake just because our understanding is eluded. Even if we can't wrap our minds around the logistics of ascension, how do we learn to talk about it? How do we let its reality shape us in the grit and grind of everyday life?

Several years ago, I began to say in my preaching that Jesus is crucified, risen, *and reigning*. Or that his work consisted of life, death, resurrection, *and* reign. Too often we stop at death and resurrection. Perhaps because resurrection is enough of a stretch. I know of plenty of churches where Easter Sunday morning sermons are prefaced with some version of, "Don't worry, we don't literally believe this stuff and you don't have to, either." As if it's much more important for us to affirm the scientific assumptions of our modern world than enter the hope that God's ways are higher and other than ours. We can't confine Jesus to a laboratory and make him do it again.

---

6. Acts 17:16.

7. "Holy mischief" is part of a previous tagline of *Geez Magazine* (https://geezmagazine.org/).

8. 1 Pet 3:15.

We have no "proof." None of us have seen anything like it, so the easy answer is to confine it to the realm of myth and metaphor and projection.

But, if we believe much of anything about God, resurrection shouldn't be that big of a deal. It seems odd that people who can look into the night sky with its countless stars, or marvel in silent wonder at a mountain range, or delight in the laughter of a newborn, and credit God with the extravagance of creation, should then be undone by resurrection. For the God of quarks and quasars, resurrection is small potatoes.[9]

That said, if we are to be taken seriously, we need to take peoples' doubts seriously. If we're to invite them into a gospel-shaped life, we need to acknowledge that we're inviting them out of a life shaped by other commitments than the things that undergird those doubts. Particularly at a time when Christian faith is one option among many, and often the weirder and more difficult one, we probably don't want to start by demanding that people start by being able to say the Apostles' Creed without their fingers crossed behind their back.

Diana Butler Bass is on to something when she argues that churches can no longer function (at least not well, or for the flourishing of faith) if we begin with particular beliefs and behaviors as prerequisite to belonging. She's right, and has the biblical backing, to say that Christian community ought to have a more belong-behave-believe rhythm to it.[10] I have a friend who says that she first showed up at a church for the community "but stayed for the Christ." That's beautiful. More of that, please.

But most of us who have been hanging around church for any length of time know that the pattern is not linear. Eventually, the things we're invited to believe and begin to take on for ourselves start to affect our behaviors and our understanding of what it means to belong to this broken and beloved body. What I believe about what's happening at the communion table and the baptismal font transforms and expands even the most generous invitation. The pattern doubles back on itself again and again. The end goal is not simply belief in the right things, but a whole-life integration of the wildly beautiful things the church has claimed and been claimed by for millennia.

Theologically speaking, the resurrection of Jesus, as a fact of history, is less an impossible miracle than the confirmation of the promise.[11] It's the

---

9. I'm indebted to Rev. Dr. Paul Scott Wilson for this insight.

10. Bass, "Great Reversal."

11. There is no satisfying sociological explanation for the life and growth of the early church when we take the literal resurrection out of the equation.

promise that the Way of Jesus is the will and way of God in the world. It's God saying, "I will have my way. The empires of the world can rage about it, the violence of the world can come in all its fury, but I will have my way. I will make this world—and everything in it—new!" The ascension is the exclamation point on the promise. It means that not only does death not win, which would be good news enough; rather, it means that the Lord of Life is on the throne of the universe. The Lamb who takes away the sin of the world is the One whose kingdom is on its way. Literally.

Another reason we don't much talk about the ascension is that, more than anything else in our liturgical calendars, it makes demands on us. Christmas reminds us of how much God wants to be with us. Easter proclaims that there is nowhere, not even hell, that God won't chase us down; there's no length to which God won't go to express divine love for us. Pentecost confirms that we are made for intimacy with God, the fiery passion of our Beloved. But the ascension insists on the best news of all: the reign of Jesus, which actually makes some demands on us. What's worse, a physical ascension—that Jesus, in his weird resurrection body, is not just vaguely raised but eternally, corporally, at the right hand of the Father—denies us the opportunity to make our faith a matter of spiritual things only. The startling claim of the ascension is that not only can heaven come to earth, but earth can go into heaven. It is the first fruits of the promise that heaven and earth really can be made one. Our unity with God will not be a one-sided matter of divine condescension. We will be raised with Christ, to dwell eternally in the glory for which we are made. It's a wild hope.

The claim of the church has been, from the beginning, that the hope of the ascended Jesus has invaded the present and is pulling us toward itself. We are in on it now. Our lives are the object of Christ's heavenward call.[12] If Jesus not only lives but also reigns, then the ascension is our enlistment notice into God's great redemption project.[13] The disciples aren't allowed to stay put, staring off into the heavens. They aren't allowed to create a shrine for eager religious tourists. They're sent off and out.

The strange thing is that, at least in the mainline, we've often celebrated that sending, while stripping it of the source of its power. We have imagined that in order to live fully in and for the world we need to abandon our more outlandish and glorious theological claims. But it seems to me that the more social justice–oriented a church is, the more we should let

12. Phil 3:14.
13. Sehested, "Ascension-Deficit."

the doctrine of the ascension work its wonder in us. Because the ascension moves our best instincts from opinion to fact. If Jesus lives and reigns, we can trust that the way he is—good news for the poor, release for the captives, fresh sight for sin-dim eyes, freedom for the oppressed, in his perfect humanity—is the way that all things will be.[14]

The ascension of Jesus allows us to take the Sermon on the Mount seriously. It is the condition under which we can fully imagine and live the truth that all relationships are being restored; that the gospel inversions that see the meek and merciful raised to glory are coming; that enemies can be treated as precious, worthy of prayer, even as we decline their dehumanizing actions; that radical generosity is the foundation of the new world God is building out of the rubble of the old. The ascension holds out the confirmation that human and divine belong together. It gives us a glimpse of the glory for which we are made, the true selves into which we are called to mature. Knowing those two things gives us an imagination for the infinite and eternal value of every other human, and the hope for the renewal of all creation.

I expect that another reason we mainliners avoid the ascension is that it causes us some theological whiplash. It implies a kind of triumphalism, and we are often at pains to avoid militaristic language and images. To say that Jesus reigns, that he is seated on the throne of the universe, and that one day every knee will bend and every tongue confess his Lordship, which will be God's glory, all of that can make our postcolonial, anti-imperial skin crawl.[15]

That concern is legitimate. We have seen the damage done when Jesus's reign is conflated with our desire for power. Our collective history is littered with evidence that religious triumphalism never seems to be good news for everybody. Mostly, it's only good for the powerful and privileged. So, it's imperative that we take seriously the beginning of Paul's hymn, in which this promise is most clearly articulated. He pleads with us to "have the same mind as Christ." Be shaped in thought and deed by the One who had everything (was equal with God!) but didn't consider that anywhere near as profitable as giving it all up for love of this world. As we proclaim Jesus's reign, we must not shy away from his call to downward mobility, the self-giving love that is at the heart of the universe.

When we call Jesus "Lord," we can only properly do so knowing that the One whose reign we sing is the One who insists that the first will be last

---

14. Luke 4:16–21.
15. Phil 2:5–11.

and the last first when his kingdom comes in all its fullness. The One whose reign we sing is the One whose flock are those who care for the sick, feed the hungry, visit the imprisoned, clothe the naked, defend the cause of the downtrodden.[16] The One whose reign we sing is the One who calls his disciples to refuse the seat of scoffers, decline the way of the powerful and self-obsessed, those whose god is their bellies, and become like children. Oddly, to grow up in Christian faith is to embrace a kind of worldly childishness.

A challenge for us mainliners is that there's a tension baked into our DNA here. From the beginning of our particular expression of Christian faith, we have often prized things like education and good social standing.[17] We don't want to be childish. We like that business leaders and local politicians sit in our pews and religiously inclined academic types take us seriously. We're glad that our preachers read the latest in biblical scholarship and are paying attention to cutting-edge scientific discoveries. In my own story, it was a successful lawyer's embrace of faith that inspired deeper spiritual digging.

None of this is inherently problematic. The early church clearly had folks from all walks of life, including the upper echelons of society. But it does make us, at least potentially, resistant to the sorts of radical things Jesus expects of his followers. We have often counted on our university-educated clergy—of which I am one—to tame Jesus's expectations and explain away any real challenge to maintaining our comfortable lives. Sometimes their jobs have depended on it.

But this is about more than gainful employment. It's about more than how our neighbors think about us. It's about more than maintaining the *status quo* that has worked out so well for many of us. It's about a constantly reinvigorated commitment to being formed with the grain of the universe, over the influence of any given culture. It's consciously deciding which version of reality we will let shape us. I heard someone say recently that there is only *intentional* spiritual formation and *unintentional* spiritual formation.[18] There is no neutrality when it comes to our spirits. The biblical witness, and the great cloud of witnesses that surrounds us, call us to unflinching formation in the way of the One whose way is making all things, even us, new. Nothing less is worthy of our God-bearing lives.

---

16. Matt 25:31–46.

17. Coffman, *Christian Century*, 5.

18. I am grateful to Tyler Staton for this insight. I heard him say this at a 24-7 Prayer Canada gathering, February 18, 2023.

Chapter 6

Within and Without

> The gifts God gave were that some would be apostles, some prophets, some evangelists, some pastors and teachers to equip the saints for the work of ministry, for building up the body of Christ until all of us come to the unity of faith and of the knowledge of the Son of God, to maturity, to the measure of the full stature of Christ.
>
> EPHESIANS 4:11–13

AT THE END OF the day, the point of the church is to equip the saints. Biblically, "saints" are not spiritual all-stars but the ordinary people who, caught up in God's grace, have elected to orient their lives in the direction of Jesus. Every one of us is called to grow into "the full stature of Christ." We are meant to equip the whole community for ministry. I do think that paid clergy play an important role, as those given the time and space to care for the words and sacraments, to be unhurried and present on behalf of a congregation, and to offer leadership for the community.[1] But the mainline dedication to ordered, seminary-educated clergy has often resulted in

---

1. In the United Church of Canada, clergy are ordained to the ministry of word, sacrament, and pastoral care; diaconal ministers are commissioned to the ministry of education, service, social justice, and pastoral care. Most mainline expressions have a similar formulation for their ministry leaders.

people outsourcing their baptismal vows to religious professionals.[2] That is an untenable pattern.

It's certainly not the case always and everywhere, but we mainliners have tended to talk more about the "ministry of all believers" than expect it, or actively equip people for it. Often in the name of welcoming, we have not expected people to embrace the growing pains of growing into Christian maturity. Spiritual disciplines and spiritual formation have been optional for quite a while. We have accepted systems that allow people to be Christians without being Christlike. We have offered Jesus without discipleship. As someone, somewhere said, "Every system is perfectly designed to get the results it gets."[3] Given our current results, we should probably reevaluate our systems.

Simon Sinek has articulated as clearly as anyone the truth that most people within most organizations know *what* is done, some know *how* it is done, and very few—if any—have a clear sense of *why* the organization does what it does.[4] I think this is an apt description of many churches. I wonder what percentage of people in an average mainline congregation, if pressed, would say that the "why" for the church is "to equip the saints, to grow people in Christian maturity, for the sake of the ministry of the body of Christ." My guess is that we would hear a lot more about community, or service, or worship. All of these are unquestionably good things for the church to do. But separated from our basic reason for being—*equipping the saints*—those things tend to lose their luster.

Lest things get too cynical, I am convinced that it's not too late. Not only that, but we also have reason to be extravagantly hopeful. As I said earlier, a miraculous number of people show up to worship every week, when they could be doing anything else. That fact alone suggests the possibility that those who are coming together Sunday after Sunday are looking for something deeper. The call of Christ is still echoing in sanctuaries and prayer rooms, in homes and offices, in the hearts of those who are choosing gospel faithfulness when no particular faith is the easier choice. Those of us who love and lead the church, professionally or not, have an obligation to respond to the fact that the Holy Spirit continues to gather people together for the specific purpose of bearing witness and giving shape to what God in Christ has done, is doing, and will do in us and for this world.

2. This is my friend Ross Lockhart's evocative phrase.
3. The source of the quote is disputed. See Deming Institute, https://deming.org/.
4. Sinek, *Start With Why*.

I know as well as anyone that how to respond to that Holy Spirit stirring can feel completely nebulous, more effort than it's worth. It's much easier to keep people mostly happy than work together to grow up into the fullness of Christ. That's why I think that Jesus's call to bear witness to repentance and the forgiveness of sins is such a gracious gift. It gives us a framework to take the life and work of our congregations, and the nurturing and upbuilding of each one of us, with holy seriousness. It also invites us to know that discipleship isn't another thing to be added to our already bloated schedules. Instead, it is a call to radical simplicity; a call to be single-minded in our pursuit of nothing short of what God wants for us, for our homes, for our communities, for this world. Jesus's invitation is for us to come to him in our weariness and trade the weight of the world for his light yoke.[5]

What's more, I think St. Peter is still right when he says that "God's divine power has given us everything needed for life and godliness, through the knowledge of him who called us by his own glory and goodness."[6] We don't have to make this up on our own. We don't have to figure out the next big strategy for church growth. We need simply to trust and lean into the promise that when God calls us to faithfulness, God equips us for that faithfulness. We have everything we need, not because of our own gifts and skills, but because we are called by the surpassing glory and goodness of Christ. That's the wellspring from which a life of repentance and the forgiveness of sins flows.

Add to that the fact that the church has some familiar resources that it has been working with fruitfully for two millennia, and we find ourselves in a place of wild and holy possibility, stats be damned. We have everything we need for a movement of people to bear world-changing, world-renewing witness to God's dream for all things. It's worth getting excited about. It's worth giving our whole selves to what God is up to in our time and place, wherever and whenever that is.

I want to insist that our contexts are fundamentally important. There is no such thing as a one-size-fits-all brand of church. The Holy Spirit is not limited to one kind of imagination for what's possible. Each of us, and each of our communities, is called to grow in awareness of the Spirit's prompting and be prepared to respond with creative faithfulness. We cannot assume

---

5. Matt 11:28. I am grateful to John Mark Comer for this reframing insight, offered at a Canadian Church Leaders Network gathering, February 17, 2023, in Vancouver, BC.

6. 2 Pet 1:3.

that what works in one community is what will work in another, or that the spiritual disciplines that enliven some will invariably enliven others. One of the more lovely realities that the four Gospels show us is that when Jesus heals someone, it's almost always different. Sometimes he speaks a word to the person, sometimes the person is nowhere near, sometimes he touches them, sometimes he rubs spit on them, sometimes they are healed immediately, and sometimes they have to walk away in trust before that healing overtakes them. I think the point is that Jesus takes individuals seriously, that what each one needs for healing and wholeness is particular. It's true for each of us as well as for our communities and congregations. Jesus's commission to embody a witness to repentance and the forgiveness of sins is an invitation to take our times and places, ourselves and each other, with divine seriousness. We must ask again and again, "What does Jesus want to do here and now?"

This is not to say that there are no consistencies across the body of Christ. If Paul's metaphor for the church holds true, then we can assume we need a measure of holistic care. I believe there are some things that we can say every Christian community needs.

Foundationally, we need regular worship and spiritual practices that point to, anticipate, embrace, and yield to the presence of God. The church is not a place where we come to be vaguely spiritual. There are lots of places to do that. The church is the place where we come to deal with the God whom we know most clearly in Jesus, by the Holy Spirit. Our worship and work need to be shaped by that fact. We need:

- Multiple kinds of spaces for people to be intentionally seeking and aware of God's presence, opportunities to "recenter our scattered senses" on the one whose desire is to have us healed and whole.

- Multiple kinds of spaces where God's healing and whole-making presence is anticipated, not just hoped for. We are promised that when we gather in Jesus's name, he will be with us, without qualification. The key, of course, is intentionally gathering *in Jesus's name*, not simply trying to tack him onto whatever we are doing.

- Worship and practices that invite people into intimacy with God, who promises to draw close. Ours is the God who is not satisfied to stay at a safe and heavenly distance, but who is eager to draw near. Ours is the God whose ways and means are far above ours, but who time and again refuses to be reduced to unknowable mystery. It would be much easier and less demanding if that were the case, but Jesus proves himself to be one who won't be hindered even by our locked doors. Indeed, he bangs on them, eager to come in and eat with us.[7] In the Mediterranean culture in which Christ spent his incarnation, eating together was a sign of intimacy and camaraderie. Jesus wants in on our lives in all his goodness and glory.

- Brave spaces to discern and yield to God's will for us and our communities. We need to be people expecting Jesus to send us as he was sent.[8] And when that happens, we need a community of co-conspirators to hold us accountable and help us live Jesus's kingdom vision in all that we do. Repentance and the forgiveness of sins are lived realities, not simply private spiritual experiences. We need support in that living.

I have already made the case that Scripture is indispensable for the life and work of the church, both individually and corporately. But let me reiterate that the point is not to overlay a rigid "plain Bible truth" on every situation as though God's word isn't living and active. The point is to develop a biblical imagination for the ways that God is at work in ourselves and our communities. The Bible is a lens through which we learn to understand not simply how things are, but how they *really* are. The Bible brings us into the company of the God who sets captives free and raises the dead; who made the world and everything in it good and very good and is fiercely determined to make it that way again; the God who calls a people to be set apart, not against the world but for it, to be a living testimony to holy love, joy, peace, patience, kindness, generosity, faithfulness, gentleness, and self-control.[9] The Bible is the primary resource for shaping us as people living for the day when all things will be made new, and all cultures will stream into the presence of God and the light of the Lamb. The Bible invites us to mature in our imaginations for that day when we will gather along the banks of the River of Life, feasting on the fruit of the Tree of Life, fresh in every season and whose leaves are for the healing of the nations. The Bible is how we know that we are about more than "pretty good news."

We need to be seeking out, creating, and engaging with resources that help us read Scripture well, so that it can shape us in the Way of Jesus. That includes good biblical criticism, and accessible resources like the Bible

---

7. Rev 3:20.
8. John 20:21.
9. Gal 5:22–23.

Project.[10] But we also need church cultures in which people are encouraged to engage deeply and prayerfully with Scripture, trusting that all the education in the world can't guarantee faithfulness. The Scriptures were written for everyday folks, not religious scholars.[11] We need good teachers, and we need to trust that the Spirit will speak to us through the Scriptures, as she has for just about ever. One of the gifts of my congregation is our annual Lenten Devotional, which is written by our members. The reflections are based off the Revised Common Lectionary for the season and offered by anyone who wants to take part. Often children will draw their reflection, people write poems, some dive deep into scholarship. Some have been hanging around for decades, others are brand new Christians. Every year I am amazed at the ways that people hear, interpret, and share the Scriptures. It is always a reminder of the gift of a multiplicity of voices when it comes to engaging God's word.[12]

As well as learning to engage and interpret the Scriptures well, we need to develop an imagination for the ways in which the Scriptures interpret us. Too often, we set ourselves up as those to whom the Bible must prove itself, and where we disagree it's obviously the Bible that has it wrong. On the one hand, I believe that the Spirit takes these ancient words and respeaks them for our time and place. Things like context and translation history are important to learn and understand so that we can hear God's voice well here and now, not just then and there. But I also believe that the Bible holds out a vision for how things are that is invariably in conflict with any culture. Returning to the Sermon on the Mount, it's beyond questioning that Jesus believes he has the authority to challenge our assumptions about the world and our place and participation in it.

Of course, we don't much like the idea of external authority over our lives these days. We are deeply suspicious of anything that smacks of power imbalances, and, more honestly, we just don't like to be told what to do. We have been trained to believe that we are the first and final arbiters of what is true and right for us, and heaven help anyone who tries to suggest otherwise. With an undergraduate degree in English language and literature, I am well-schooled in reading with a "hermeneutic of suspicion." This is a way of reading and interpreting any kind of media with a baseline of skepticism, always on the lookout for hidden or subversive ways in which

---

10. Bible Project, "Messiah."
11. Peterson, *Eat This Book*, 141.
12. University Hill Congregation, "Lenten Devotionals."

we as readers are being manipulated. A hermeneutic of suspicion assumes some intention other than what is being revealed, usually toward some nefarious end. It was the primary mode of interpretation throughout my undergrad, and because it pervades so much of academia, it showed up regularly throughout my seminary training.

A hermeneutic of suspicion is certainly not without merit when we approach Scripture. For instance, we might rightly ask why one version of King David's story contains the Bathsheba disaster, and one doesn't. It's worth asking why in one letter, Paul can sing that there is now "no male or female" in Christ, and in another can clearly articulate a hierarchy of genders.[13] Is one the later addition of patriarchal leaders in the early development of the church? Or do we acknowledge that Paul is simply a product of his time and dismiss his instructions as historical relics? Or do we try to dig in behind the text and figure out why Paul would tell Timothy not to allow women to teach? When something so clearly grates against our understanding of the world, it is worth taking a step back to see what the Spirit has to say about it now. The internal corrections and conversations within Scripture itself should keep us from swallowing the whole thing uncritically. In the mainline we are fond of boasting that we don't have to leave our brains at the door.

However, I would suggest that in our preaching and teaching, in our study and devotions, we really ought to start with a hermeneutic of trust. Though I often wish God would have chosen a more reliable vessel than human witness and testimony to tell the divine story, I also want to learn to trust that my ancestors and siblings in faith were striving to be as faithful as they could be. I want to begin by trusting that the Holy Spirit can take our feeble human offerings and breathe them into truth. I want to trust that God really does desire our freedom and flourishing and will not ask us to do anything that would work against that—even when it's not immediately clear how, for example, something like loving our enemies and praying for our persecutors could possibly be worth doing. I want to trust that the Scriptures that have nourished a countercultural faithfulness in Israel and the church for thousands of years can do the same for us, here and now.

One of the primary ways we develop a hermeneutic of trust is through prayer. If Jesus's promise is true, that he is the Good Shepherd and his sheep know his voice, then we need prayer practices that help us both recognize

---

13. Gal 3:28; 1 Tim 2:12.

that voice and trust more and more in his goodness.[14] Prayer is the primary means by which we respond to the word through which we are made. It is the way in which we develop intimacy with the One who is most intimate with us.

Prayer is analogous to the relationship-building communication in any relationship. If I were to tell the married couples in my congregation to stop talking to one another, and instead come once a week and I'll tell them all about each other—what lovely people they are, how creative and interesting, how much affection they have for one another—no one would take that seriously. We know full well that we can't have a relationship with someone about whom we only have information and no interaction. And yet, this seems to be a common pattern for how people relate to God. Prayer is the way in which our head knowledge—what we know about God—becomes our heart knowledge—how we live with God.

Unfortunately, many people find the idea of prayer overwhelming, and we have not always done a good job of equipping them to overcome that. There are simple ways to get into prayer, through practices like *lectio divina*, or Ignatian spiritual practices that are easily found on the internet.[15] I am fond of apps like Pray as You Go, or Lectio 365, which offer short, guided meditations on Scripture, often with themes connected to the church calendar.[16]

I have also come to appreciate the guidance of Rich Villodas when it comes to prayer. He counsels us to:

- **Befriend Silence**: If we want to enjoy God's presence, we need to find time and space away from distractions, and we need to stop talking at least some of the time. Like any relationship, if we are going to exchange presence, we need to leave room for one another.
- **Normalize Boredom**: In a relationship of intimacy, not every moment can be full of fiery passion. Sometimes it's enough to know that my wife is nearby, and we can both relax in each other's presence, accomplishing nothing.
- **Pray Using the Words of Others**: There are no points for authenticity when it comes to prayer. What's more, there are plenty of times when

---

14. John 10:11–18.

15. Upper Room has several accessible guides to different types of prayer practice: https://www.upperroom.org/.

16. https://www.24-7prayer.com/resource/lectio-365/; https://pray-as-you-go.org/.

our words fail, and the prayers of others can give us a way to express what's going on in our hearts and lives. The psalms, the prayerbook of the Bible, are an invaluable addition to any spiritual practice.[17]

- **Remember that God Is Looking at You in Love**: Again and again Scripture invites us to "approach the throne of mercy boldly," to come to God as our divine parent who loves to give their children good gifts. God delights in you. Pray knowing that.[18]

Prayer is how we lean into our reconciled relationship with God. It's also how we begin to bear witness to both repentance and the forgiveness of sins, our call to be reconciled in all our relationships. An essential part of any praying life is confession. It is the means by which we acknowledge that we have not loved God or what God loves with all we've got. It is a conscious act of humility, recognizing that we have fallen short of the glory for which we are made.

Every bit as important as confession is absolution, or the assurance of grace—the proclamation of forgiveness.[19] Confession and absolution as a regular, formative practice is one of the most important gifts we have to offer as communities being shaped in the Way of Jesus. Ellen Davis, preaching on the resurrection narrative in the Gospel of John, insists that "forgiveness of sins is the foundational mission of the church, as John sees it."[20] She continues:

> Through the Holy Spirit, Jesus is granting humans a power that previously belonged to God alone: the power to unlock the death grip that our sins have on our souls, to erase them from the cosmos. The power to forgive sins is the mark of a new creation, of a profoundly changed life not just for this small group of disciples, but potentially for humankind altogether.[21]

In the Way of Jesus, we do have a choice: forgive sins or retain them. But in the wake of Jesus, that's a lopsided choice. The balance tips invariably and eternally toward forgiveness. If we are caught up with the Spirit who grows in us the fruit of generosity and faithfulness, we can assume that those fruits take shape in a prodigal forgiveness of sin. The church

---

17. See Taylor, *Open and Unafraid*.
18. Villodas, *Deeply Formed*, 22–28.
19. Smith, *You Are What You Love*, 109–10.
20. Davis, "Learning to Believe," para 13; John 20:21–23.
21. Davis, "Learning to Believe," para 10.

should be a place where we are made aware of our sin, not so that we can be weighed down by it, but so that we can give it up to the God who can do something about it. The goal of Christian confession is always freedom. Some of our most joyful work is calling one another back into the presence of the One "who is able to keep you from falling, and to make you stand without blemish in the presence of his glory with rejoicing!"[22]

It's as we grow in confidence of our gracious standing in the presence of God's glory that we begin to understand what it means to be called "saints." The Christian Scriptures are clear that our sainthood is not the result of anything that we have done, or relative to our behavior. Paul regularly calls his congregations "saints" and then tears a strip off them for living decidedly unsaintly lives, because sainthood is a new life we inhabit through and in response to the grace of Christ. To be a saint is simply to be part of that great cloud of witnesses learning to be the first fruits of God's new creation, one step, one relationship, one day at a time. To "build up the saints" is to help one another live fully and freely in the name and Way of Jesus, whatever we do, for the glory of God.[23]

The shorthand for that way of life is *discipleship*. Discipleship is the path we walk toward our True Selves, becoming the people we are fearfully and wonderfully made to be.[24] And it's the way that we bear witness to repentance—wholehearted commitment to the politics of Jesus. Disciples are people learning to do what their teacher does, developing the mind of Christ through lifelong apprenticeship, discovering the rhythms and movements of Christ so that they become perfectly natural. *Lifelong* is the key here. This is about more than saying a Sinner's Prayer or responding to an altar call at summer camp. It is life lived in joyful response to our absolution.

Again, this isn't adding *another thing to do*. It is a new way of being in the world, not tossed about by the demands of a culture that is constantly disintegrating us. It's an intentional commitment to deciding who and what gets to shape our spirits. Will it be the demands of an individualistic, consumeristic, depersonalizing, worldly insistence that our lives are happy accidents with which we are free to do as we please? Or will we come to the One who has come alongside us, whose word is life, who made us and knows us better than we know ourselves, and whose deepest desire is for

22. Jude 1:24.
23. Col 3:17.
24. Ps 139:14.

our good? Will we define ourselves by the newsreels, by things that rust and rot and fade away, by the opinions and standards of a world that regularly seems to be going off the rails? Or will we build a life on the words of the One whose word is sure, the foundation of life that is truly life? None of us are as self-defined as we are encouraged to imagine. We can't live without reference to others. So, who will be our primary reference, the Morning Star that guides us in the way of surpassing peace, or someone or something else? That's what we're asking when it comes to discipleship.

Another challenge for many of us is that the way of discipleship is invariably communal and accountable. By design, we can't do it alone. This can be difficult because people can be difficult. Worse, growing together demands a kind of vulnerability that many of us have spent a lot of time steeling ourselves against. We have accepted the lie that faith is a private matter. But there's a reason that the backbone of most large (often more evangelical) churches is a network of small groups, designed for intimacy and intentional, mutual discipleship: disciples are made in community. The Way of Jesus is unflinchingly relational. His first act of ministry was to gather a crew of fellow travelers, set apart so that they could be trained in a new way of being, *together*. He knew that the surest way to decrease in faith and stumble in discipleship is to try to do it alone, challenging as other people might be.

The flip side of the challenge of growi sng in faith relationally, is that we *get* to do it relationally. We do not have to sort this life out on our own. We can learn with and from others, we can teach those who are new to faith. We can encourage each other, inviting each other deeper in faith and supporting each other in holy riskiness. We get to, as Paul says, weep with those who are weeping, hoping together in that day when every tear will be wiped away.[25] We get to share in each other's joys, learning to delight in the wonders that infuse every life. We get to confess to one another, often discovering that our struggles are not much different than anyone else's. And we get to proclaim grace and forgiveness over one another, giving voice and witness to the truth that we are caught up with the One who is eager to cleanse us of all unrighteousness.[26]

What's more, communal discernment is much richer than individual discernment. Praying together, reading Scripture together, paying attention to the needs of the community together, means that we are not limited by

---

25. Rev 21:4; Rom 12:15.
26. 1 John 1:9.

our own narrow field of vision. We can draw on the wisdom of others. We can count on their support to do the hard things that Jesus calls us to do. Though the call is for each of us to pick up our own crosses—live our particular lives of holy rebellion against the death-dealing ways of the world, as the beloved and God-bearing people that we are—it is my experience that carrying our crosses together makes them seem somehow lighter. In the same way that working out with a partner increases not only the likelihood of showing up to the gym, but often encourages us to push a little harder, so training in righteousness together increases our commitments and invites us to trust that ours is the God who will do *more* in us and through us than we can ask or imagine.

Coming together to do the things that Jesus calls us to do also means that we can listen for God's call into the world together. The goal of communal discipleship is not withdrawal and insularity. Jesus tells his disciples that they are to bear witness to repentance and the forgiveness of sins "to all nations, beginning from Jerusalem." We are called to pay attention and respond to the communities around us, moving ever farther into the world. This requires a contextual analysis that demands more than individual voices. We can and must work together to pay attention to where we are out of right relationship with others, within the congregation certainly, but also outside of it, in our everyday lives. Who are we being called to share the good news of repentance and forgiveness of sins with, individually and as a community, and how are we to do that sharing? What will the shape of our witness be, specifically, tangibly, practically? What resources, spiritually and otherwise, do we need in order to respond in faithfulness to the people God is calling us to serve?

Because we are meant to flourish in all four key relationships for which we are created, we ought to be asking these questions not just about the people around us, but also the places we find ourselves in, and all our nonhuman neighbors. As stewards of God's good creation, we have an obligation to consider how we are called to grow in humble service of the whole created order. The church should be a place where we learn to delight in the gift of this world, its intricacy and beauty, marveling at our interconnectedness and interdependence with all living things. One way to do that is to get outside together. The Wild Church Network is a movement of Christians who invite us to return to nature as a spiritual practice.[27] They provide resources and encouragement for a variety of ways to worship and

---

27. Wild Church Network, https://www.wildchurchnetwork.com/.

learn together, rooting our discipleship in the particular places we live. *A Rocha*, a "family of Christian conservation organizations," has sites all over the world, where people come together to do important environmental work, learn about the land they live on, and grow in their commitment to tend to God's beloved creation.

One of the things I especially love about *A Rocha* is their commitment to serious and worshipful conservation work, where they are with what they've got.[28] Although the work is not always easy, and the headlines can be deflating, my experience is that these organizations embody a radical and intentional hopefulness. Climate change is an unquestionably urgent concern for life on earth, and should be especially so for those of us called to proclaim repentance and forgiveness of sin. But it is easy to be overwhelmed by the magnitude of the emergency. Trusting in Jesus's promise that small things done for the sake of his kingdom will yield more than we can imagine or expect, *A Rocha* and folks all over the world of a similar mind do that important Christian work of provoking us to goodness.[29] We can do the same in our places and communities, provoking one another beyond the "pretty good news" that we're still here, to the staggeringly good news that we are called and claimed by the One who is making all things new.

---

28. Kostamo, *Planted*.
29. Heb 10:24.

Conclusion

Although taking seriously Jesus's commission to bear witness to repentance and the forgiveness of sins might require some significant changes in the way we do things—and we don't much like to change—I think we have recently been shown that we can do that when we have to. The COVID-19 pandemic demonstrated that when we recognize an urgent need to do things differently, we have the capacity to do so quickly and effectively. On March 8, 2020, it was unclear what it would look like to worship under pandemic conditions in the months ahead. By March 15, 2020, most of Canada had shut down all public gatherings. The lockdown radically changed how we could worship together. We had to learn new skills quickly. We adapted to a circumstance none of us had ever faced, and many churches did it well. From my contacts across the country and around the world, I know that congregations practiced a kind of contextual analysis, and did what was appropriate for their communities, with what they had. It was, for me, evidence that "we've never done that before" is no longer a reason not to do things differently.

In many ways what I have written is an exercise in articulating what I think we are called to as Christians, and what I think the church could be. If you came to my current congregation, you would see some of what's above, and you would find other areas where we clearly have work to do. We live by grace, after all. But I can't help but wonder what it would look like to have mainline churches across North America taking seriously Jesus's commission to bear witness to repentance and the forgiveness of sins. Can we imagine the harvest if congregations—regardless of size (two or three of us gathered in Jesus's name is enough), or budget (the widow's mite is a kingdom-sized investment), with or without ordained clergy, whatever their history or their prospects for the future—were intentional about maturing in Christ, relentless in walking in his way, and embracing forgiveness of sins, the reconciliation of all relationships, as our missional purpose. I think it would be extraordinary.

Let me repeat my conviction that St. Peter is right: we have everything we need for life and godliness, the abundance and flourishing for which we are made. Next time you gather for worship, look around and take in the miracle of what's happening. The Spirit of the Living God has gathered this group of people, who could be doing anything else, to come together in worship, to sit under the Scriptures, to sing of a wild hope, to say again that we and this whole blessed world belong to God. And in Christ, God is taking it back, healing it, and making it new. It's an audacious thing that happens every Sunday. Imagine if we let that holy audacity find shape in all we do.

The fact is, that's how God's kingdom has always advanced, with little groups of relative nobodies committing themselves to the Way of Jesus and inviting others to do the same. It's notable that we hardly know anything about the churches in the New Testament, and only a handful of names from those communities. Of those named, most we don't know anything more than that. One of my favorite characters in all of Scripture is Simon the Tanner. We know two things about him, besides his name: he was a tanner, and he let Peter stay at his place for a while. What we also know is that this simple act of hospitality played a crucial part in the transformation of the early church, without which most of us wouldn't be a part of it.[1] The enduring gift of the mainline is that we are full of people like Simon the Tanner, ready to open their doors in the name of Jesus, trusting that it just might change the world. Or at least a life.

It was in a little United Church of Canada congregation, in the middle of nowhere—my first charge, in Selkirk, Ontario—where I really learned to read the Bible in community. The congregation of Faith Centennial United Church taught me that all the fancy words I learned in seminary don't amount to much if they don't have to do with what happens in the barn, or the classroom, or driving a combine, or at the local diner. Kris and Robert Kerfont modelled easy Christian hospitality. As important as anything, Faith Centennial taught me to pray in community. Sue Webb and Mairi Mowat and others taught me at every Wednesday morning prayer meeting, what "a long obedience in the same direction" looks like.[2]

---

1. Acts 10:5–6.
2. Peterson, *Long Obedience*.

CONCLUSION

It was Karen McSpadden who first encouraged me to lead in Sunday School, and Bob Stubbs showed me what simple, steady faith looks like, at Norwich United Church, in Norwich, Ontario. It was countless potlucks and Christmas pageants and my confirmation class that solidified the truth that faith is not a solo adventure in spiritual escapism. It has to be done on the ground, in the thick and thin of life, together.

It was Meredith Jackson Donohue's leadership in the Alpha Course, at First-Grantham United Church, in St. Catharines, Ontario, who made the space for me to hear God's call to ministry at a critical time. To hear an accomplished lawyer, with what seemed like all the material and professional advantages and blessings one could want, say that exploring her faith and encountering Jesus was the most important thing she ever did, was a mind-expanding possibility for me.

The first picture of me in the pulpit is from when I was four years old, at Trinity United Church, in Vankleek Hill, Ontario, where my dad was the minister.

The congregation that I serve and am part of now, University Hill Congregation, has been a space of grace and encouragement as I've tried to mature a little more deeply into this "odd and wondrous calling."[3] On the campus of the University of British Columbia, we're a strange witness to God's grace, in a strange place to do ministry—and they've been doing it for generations.

I have no doubt that I could have been well shaped in faith elsewhere, in some other tradition. But experience tells me that it would have been different. *I* would be different without these churches. Explaining exactly why or how is like trying to explain the taste of a peach to someone who's never had one. The only way to do it properly is to give them a peach—preferably a Niagara peach.

That's why this limb of the body matters to me, and why I am relentlessly hopeful that if we are willing, God will do more in us and through us than we can ask or imagine. May it be so.

---

3. Daniel and Copenhaver, *Odd and Wondrous*.

Bibliography

Acts and Proceedings of the One Hundred and Forty-Seventh General Assembly of the Presbyterian Church in Canada. The Presbyterian Church in Canada, June 5–8, 2022. presbyterian.ca.

Alpha Canada. https://alphacanada.org/.

Barna Group. "Only 10% of Christian Twentysomethings Have Resilient Faith." September 24, 2019. https://www.barna.com/research/of-the-four-exile-groups-only-10-are-resilient-disciples/.

Bass, Diana Butler. "The Great Reversal." *Life Long Faith* 5.4 (2011) 3–7. https://www.lifelongfaith.com/uploads/5/1/6/4/5164069/great_reversal_-_bass.pdf.

Bell, Steve. "Symphony and Trinity." Steve Bell blog. https://web.archive.org/web/20200926191623/https://stevebell.com/symphony-and-trinity/.

Bennett, David, and Ashley John Moyse. "Learning Personhood Again: The Importance of the Trinity for Understanding Our Personal Humanity." *Touchstone* 39.2 (2021) 6–14.

The Bible Project. "Messiah." Video, 5:48. September 30, 2014. https://bibleproject.com/explore/video/messiah/.

"Billie Eilish Says Watching Porn as a Child 'Destroyed My Brain.'" *The Guardian*, December 14, 2021. https://www.theguardian.com/music/2021/dec/15/billie-eilish-says-watching-porn-gave-her-nightmares-and-destroyed-my-brain.

Buechner, Frederick. "The Final Secret." Frederick Buechner blog, June 19, 2019. https://www.frederickbuechner.com/quote-of-the-day/2019/6/19/the-final-secret.

———. *Telling the Truth: The Gospel as Tragedy, Comedy and Fairytale*. San Francisco: HarperSanFrancisco, 1977.

Byassee, Jason. *Trinity: The God We Don't Know*. Nashville: Abingdon, 2015.

Carpenter, Chris. "The Gospel According to Starbucks." *CBN*, December 10, 2022. https://www1.cbn.com/biblestudy/the-Gospel-according-to-starbucks.

Chesterton, G. K. *What's Wrong With the World*. San Francisco: Ignatius, 2014.

Choucri, Nazli, ed. "Global Environmental Accord: Strategies for Sustainability and Institutional Innovation." n.d. https://mitpress.mit.edu/series/global-environmental-accord-strategies-for-sustainability-and-institutional-innovation/.

Claiborne, Shane. *The Irresistible Revolution: Living as an Ordinary Radical*. Grand Rapids: Zondervan, 2006.

Claiborne, Shane, and Chris Haw. *Jesus for President*. Grand Rapids: Zondervan, 2009.

Coffman, Elesha J. *The Christian Century and the Rise of the Protestant Mainline*. New York: Oxford University Press, 2013.

BIBLIOGRAPHY

Creasy Dean, Kenda, and Ron Foster. *The God-bearing Life: The Art of Soul Tending for Youth Ministry*. Nashville: Upper Room, 1998.

Daniel, Lillian, and Martin B. Copenhaver. *This Odd and Wondrous Calling: The Public and Private Lives of Two Ministers* Grand Rapids: William B Eerdmans, 2009.

Davis, Ellen F. "Learning to Believe." Faith and Leadership, April 25, 2010. https://faithandleadership.com/learning-believe.

Davis, Pete. *Dedicated: The Case for Commitment in an Age of Infinite Browsing*. New York: Avid Reader, 2021.

The Deming Institute. https://deming.org.

Dickau, Tim. *Forming Christian Communities in a Secular Age: Recovering Humility and Hope*. Toronto: Tyndale Academic, 2021.

Doyle, Brian. *One Long River of Song: Notes on Wonder*. New York: Bay Back, 2019.

Duhan-Kaplan, Laura. *Mouth of the Donkey: Reimagining Biblical Animals*. Eugene, OR: Cascade, 2021.

Florer-Bixler, Melissa. *How to Have an Enemy: Righteous Anger and the Work of Peace*. Harrisonburg: Herald, 2021.

Gibson, Helen. "How Much Do Evangelicals Actually Engage with Scripture?" Lifeway Research, June 5, 2018. https://lifewayresearch.com/2018/06/05/how-do-evangelicals-really-engage-with-scripture/.

Guite, Malcolm. *Faith, Hope and Poetry: Theology and the Poetic Imagination*. Farnham: Ashgate, 2010.

———. *Waiting on the Word: A Poem a Day for Advent, Christmas and Epiphany*. Norwich: Canterbury, 2015.

Harper, Lisa Sharon. *The Very Good Gospel: How Everything Wrong Can be Made Right*. Colorado Springs: Waterbrook, 2016.

Harris, Daniel. "Mulholland: 'In God for the World.'" SalvationLife, May 10, 2018. http://www.salvationlife.com/blog/mulholland-in-god-for-the-world.

Heschel, Abraham Joshua. "Radical Amazement." Awakin, n.d. https://www.awakin.org/v2/read/view.php?tid=1080.

Hickman, Martha. *How to Marry a Minister*. Philadelphia: J. B. Lippincott, 1966.

Horowitz, Alexandra. *On Looking: A Walker's Guide to the Art of Observation*. New York: Scribner, 2013.

Hughes, Robert. "The Shock of the New, episode 2—The Powers that Be." YouTube, 58:39, March 14, 2014. https://www.youtube.com/watch?v=3JEx6CDW6-0.

Jennings, Willie James. *Acts*. Louisville: Westminster John Knox, 2017.

John Paul II, Pope. "Creation Reveals God's Glory." Interdisciplinary Encyclopedia of Religion and Science, March 12, 1986. https://inters.org/John-Paul-II-Catechesis-Creation-Glory.

Keesmaat, Sylvia C., and Brian J. Walsh. *Romans Disarmed: Resisting Empire, Demanding Justice*. Grand Rapids: Brazos, 2019.

Kostamo, Leah. *Planted: A Story of Creation, Calling, and Community*. Eugene, OR: Cascade, 2013.

"Mahatma Gandhi Says He Believes in Christ but Not Christianity." *The Harvard Crimson*, January 11, 1927. https://www.thecrimson.com/article/1927/1/11/mahatma-gandhi-says-he-believes-in/.

Moberly, R. W. L. *Old Testament Theology: Reading the Hebrew Bible as Christian Scripture*. Grand Rapids: Baker Academic, 2013.

Moltmann, Jürgen. *The Church in the Power of the Spirit*. New York: Harper & Row, 1977.

BIBLIOGRAPHY

Mullins, Matthew. *Enjoying the Bible: Literary Approaches to Loving the Scriptures.* Grand Rapids: Baker Academic, 2021.

Myers, Ben. *The Apostles' Creed: A Guide to the Ancient Catechism.* Bellingham, WA: Lexham, 2018.

Nouwen, Henri J. M. *In the Name of Jesus: Reflections on Christian Leadership.* New York: Crossroad, 1989.

Perrin, Ruth. *Changing Shape: The Faith Lives of Millennials.* London: SCM, 2020.

Peterson, Eugene H. *Eat This Book: A Conversation In the Art of Spiritual Reading.* Grand Rapids: William B. Eerdmans, 2006.

———. *A Long Obedience in the Same Direction: Discipleship in an Instant Society.* 2nd ed. Downers Grove, IL: InterVarsity, 2000.

———. *Practice Resurrection: A Conversation on Growing Up in Christ.* Grand Rapids: William B. Eerdmans, 2010.

Pouteaux, Preston. *The Bees of Rainbow Falls: Finding Faith, Imagination, and Delight in Your Neighbourhood.* Skyforest, CA: Urban Loft, 2017.

Root, Andrew. "The End of Youth Ministry." *When the Church Stops Working*, podcast, episode 14, March 31, 2020.

———. *Faith Formation in a Secular Age: Responding to the Church's Obsession with Youthfulness.* Grand Rapids: Baker Academic, 2017.

———. *The Pastor in a Secular Age: Ministry to People Who No Longer Need a God.* Grand Rapids: Baker Academic, 2019.

Rowe, C. Kavin. *Christianity's Surprise: A Sure and Certain Hope.* Nashville: Abingdon, 2020.

———. *World Upside Down: Reading Acts in the Graeco-Roman Age.* New York: Oxford University Press, 2009.

Scandrette, Mark. *Practicing the Way of Jesus: Life Together in the Kingdom of Love.* Downers Grove, IL: InterVarsity, 2011.

Sehested, Ken. "Ascension-Deficit Disorder: A Meditation on the Feast of the Ascension." *Prayer and Politiks*, 2021. https://prayerandpolitiks.org/articles-essays-sermons/ascension-deficit-disorder/.

Sinek, Simon. *Start With Why: How Great Leaders Inspire Everyone to Take Action.* New York: Portfolio, 2009.

Smith, James K. A. *How to Inhabit Time: Understanding the Past, Facing the Future, Living Faithfully Now.* Grand Rapids: Brazos, 2022.

———. *You Are What You Love: The Spiritual Power of Habit.* Grand Rapids: Brazos, 2016.

Taylor, Charles. *A Secular Age.* Cambridge: Belknap, 2007.

Taylor, W. David O. *Open and Unafraid: The Psalms as a Guide for Life.* Nashville: Nelson, 2020.

Thompson, Curt. *The Soul of Shame: Retelling the Stories We Believe About Ourselves.* Downers Grove, IL: InterVarsity, 2015.

———. "What Is Shame?" YouTube, 42:17, January 21, 2020. https://www.youtube.com/watch?v=_goX9vPp-V4.

"Truth and Reconciliation Commission of Canada." Government of Canada, September 29, 2022. https://www.rcaanc-cirnac.gc.ca/eng/1450124405592/1529106060525/

United Church of Canada. "A New Creed (1968)." https://united-church.ca/community-faith/welcome-united-church-canada/faith-statements/new-creed-1968.

BIBLIOGRAPHY

University Hill Congregation. "Lenten Devotionals." https://uhillcongregation.squarespace.com/lenten-devotionals.

The Upper Room. https://www.upperroom.org.

Villodas, Rich. *Deeply Formed Life: Five Transformative Values to Root Us in the Way of Jesus*. Colorado Springs: Waterbrook, 2020.

———. Twitter, July 10, 2021.

Wallace, David Foster. "Big Red Son." In *Consider the Lobster and Other Essays*, 3–50. New York: Little, Brown and Company, 2005.

Wesley, Charles. "Hymns for Ascension-Day, Hymn 1." In *Ascension Hymns (1746)*, edited by Randy L. Maddox, updated September 3, 2007, 3–4. https://divinity.duke.edu/sites/divinity.duke.edu/files/documents/cswt/36_Ascension_Hymns_%281746%29.pdf.

"What Is Redemptive Entrepreneurship?" Praxis, n.d. https://www.praxislabs.org/redemptive-entrepreneurship.

White, James Emery. *Meet Generation Z: Understanding and Reaching the New Post-Christian World*. Grand Rapids: Baker, 2017.

Wild Church Network. https://www.wildchurchnetwork.com/.

Willimon, William H. *Undone by Easter: Keeping Preaching Fresh*. Nashville: Abingdon, 2009.

Winner, Lauren. *The Danger of Christian Practice: On Wayward Gifts, Characteristic Damage, and Sin*. New Haven: Yale University Press, 2018.

Wright, N. T. *Jesus and the Victory of God: Christian Origins and the Question of God*. Christian Origins and the Question of God, vol. 2. Minneapolis: Fortress, 1996.

Yaconelli, Mike. "Spirituality Made Hard." Interview with Dallas Willard. *The Door Magazine* 129 (May/June 1993). https://dwillard.org/articles/spirituality-made-hard.

www.ingramcontent.com/pod-product-compliance
Lightning Source LLC
Chambersburg PA
CBHW030901170426
43193CB00009BA/701